P9-DVV-982

1001 IDEAS FOR
BATHROOMS
The Ultimate Sourcebook

1001 IDEAS FOR
BATHROOMS
The Ultimate Sourcebook

Fixtures, Accessories,
and Decorative Treatments

JERRI FARRIS

Creative Publishing
international

First published in North America in 2008 by
Creative Publishing International
400 First Avenue North
Suite 300
Minneapolis, MN 55401
800 328 3895
www.creativepub.com

Creative Publishing
international

Copyright © 2008 Marshall Editions
All rights reserved

A Marshall Edition
Conceived, edited, and designed by
Marshall Editions
The Old Brewery
6 Blundell Street
London N7 9BH
U.K.
www.marshalleditions.com

For Marshall Editions:
Publisher: Richard Green
Art Director: Ivo Marloh
Commissioning Editor: Claudia Martin
Managing Editor: Paul Docherty
Project Editor: Amy Head
Design and editorial: Seagull Design
Indexer: Lisa Footitt
Production: Nikki Ingram

For Creative Publishing international:
President/CEO: Ken Fund
VP for Sales & Marketing: Kevin Hamric
Publisher: Bryan Trandem
Managing Editor: Tracy Stanley
Editor: Jennifer Gehlhar
Production Managers: Linda Halls, Laura Hokkanen
Creative Director: Michele Lanci-Altomare
Senior Design Managers: Jon Simpson, Brad Springer
Design Managers: Sara Holle, James Kegley

Copyright under International, Pan American, and Universal
Copyright Conventions. All rights reserved. No part of this
book may be reproduced or transmitted in any form or by any
means, electronic or mechanical, including photocopying,
recording, or by any information storage-and-retrieval system,
without written permission from the copyright holder.

ISBN-10: 1-58923-419-7
ISBN-13: 987-1-58923-419-2

A catalog record for this book is available from the
Library of Congress

Current printing (last digit)
10 9 8 7 6 5 4 3 2 1

Originated in Hong Kong by Modern Age
Printed and bound in China

Front cover image: Eric Roth
Back cover image: Duravit

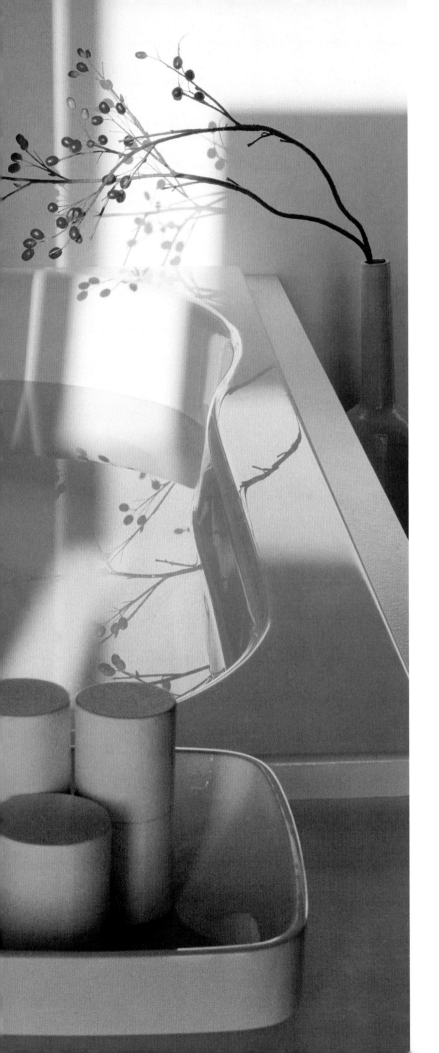

Contents

Introduction

Trend watchers report that large, luxurious bathrooms are the second most requested feature by home buyers. Only kitchens are more critical to a home's appeal. This can hardly be considered surprising. More than a third of the population reports experiencing extreme stress on an ongoing basis. In today's fast-paced society, people want—no, they need—a place to relax and pamper themselves. More and more often, that place is the bathroom.

The bathroom is the last frontier of personal privacy. In our constantly connected world, where communication is so advanced we rarely have a moment to ourselves, most people still hesitate to disturb someone in the bathroom. That simple truth is one of the main reasons so many homeowners long to create spa-like atmospheres in their bathrooms: behind the closed door lies peace and quiet.

According to national real-estate surveys, bathrooms have steadily increased in size over the past 30 years. The average bathroom built today is twice as large as the average bathroom in a home built in the 1970s. These statistics play a large part in the growing bathroom renovation trend. A home with at least one large, luxurious bathroom is worth substantially more than one with comparable square footage and merely average bathrooms.

Remodeling a bathroom is generally considered a wise investment. A recent cost-versus-value survey indicates that a remodeled upscale bathroom delivers at least a 77 percent return on your investment. In other words, if you sold your house within a year of completing the project, you'd get approximately 77 cents out of every dollar you invested in it. The rate of return is even greater if you're adding a master bath to a home that didn't have one or a second bathroom to a home with only one full bath.

All these facts and figures are valuable and should have an impact on decisions about remodeling or adding bathrooms. However, they cannot be the sole determining factors. Instead, the heart of the matter is whether you want to invest the time and money required to design, plan, and guide the construction of a more opulent bathroom. Remodeling or adding a bathroom can be a long process filled with products to research and select, issues to resolve, and no small level of inconvenience to endure. In the end, the one true test of whether a project makes sense is whether you believe you will enjoy the results enough to justify that process. Only you and your family can answer that question.

Opposite: Custom showers, such as this, are among the most desired amenities in bathrooms today.

Below: Double sinks are welcome additions to master baths and other bathrooms used by more than one person at a time.

Evaluating Your Bathroom

Before beginning a bathroom remodeling project, the first step is to evaluate the current room. Here are some questions to ask yourself. The answers will guide your decision as well as the planning process if you decide to go ahead with the project.

- Is the room large enough?
- Does it include fixtures that appeal to you?
- Are the current fixtures safe? For example, does the shower have a non-slip floor and regulated controls? Are the bathtub controls within reach from outside the tub?
- Is there enough storage?
- Are the furnishings, including the cabinets, attractive and in good condition?
- Is the lighting and ventilation adequate? Attractive? Comfortable?
- Do you enjoy spending time there?

If you answer no to more than three or four of these questions, it probably makes sense to remodel the room. Take note of the elements you are satisfied with and those you think need improvement when planning your new bathroom.

① Today's master suites combine the finest fixtures and materials to provide incredible levels of luxury. This large bath includes a soaking tub and shower as well as a state-of-the-art toilet and bidet and striking sink.

② Natural materials, multiple levels, and oversized fixtures are the hallmarks of this contemporary bathroom. Note that the fireplace is positioned on the wall so bathers can view the flames while reclining in the tub.

③ If a spa atmosphere appeals to you, why not go all the way? Inspired by Asian influences, this bathroom offers a peaceful oasis to relax and unwind.

④ All eyes are drawn to the deep soaking tub in the center of this sparkling bathroom.

Planning Your Bathroom

Planning a bathroom project starts with answering two simple questions: how much space and how much money can you devote to the project? The answers impact, directly or indirectly, the selection of virtually everything in the room, including fixtures, fittings, and finish materials.

Adding square footage is a more involved, more expensive undertaking than remodeling existing space. However, if the current space can't be reconfigured to serve your needs, dressing it up is unlikely to produce the results you want. Measure your room and do some research on the space requirements for the fixtures you want before moving to the next stage of the planning process.

Once you've devised a budget for the project, the planning process can really take off. Much of it is a matter of fitting the elements you want into the available space and budget.

When it comes to planning a remodeling project, thorough research is essential. You'll find a great deal of valuable information in the pages of this book. The Internet, manufacturers' catalogs and brochures, and retail showrooms are other important sources of information. It's a good idea to consult a designer or contractor while you're still in the early stages of planning your project.

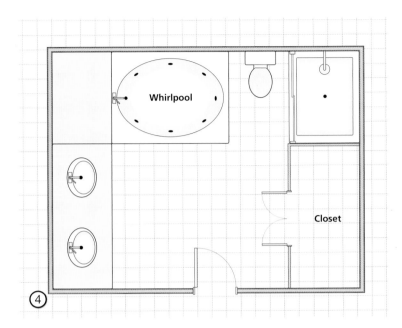

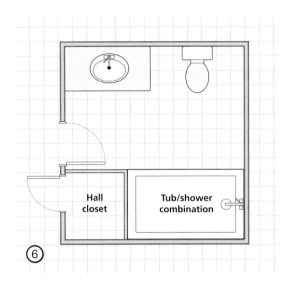

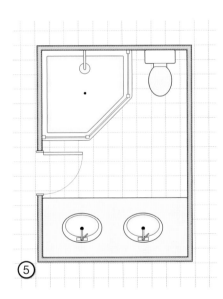

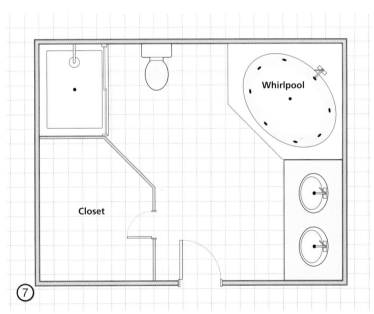

① Small spaces can host exceptional bathrooms when they're planned to make the most of every square foot.

② Medium-sized spaces can be fitted with architectural details and elegant fixtures to create inviting, comfortable environments.

③ Large bathrooms can be configured to provide every possible luxury.

④ The layout for this master bath includes a whirlpool tub, corner shower, double sinks, and a walk-in closet that also serves as a dressing area.

⑤ A large, luxurious shower and double sinks are tucked into this family bath.

⑥ The layout for this guest bath includes a shower/bath combination as well as a sink and vanity. The linen closet is accessed from the hall.

⑦ Placing the whirlpool tub, walk-in closet, and shower in the corners leaves plenty of open space in the center, creating a master bath that is airy and easy to use.

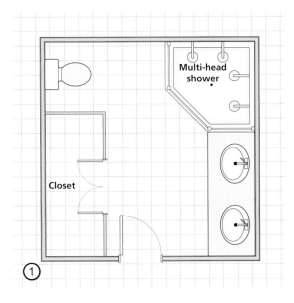

Multi-head shower

Closet

①

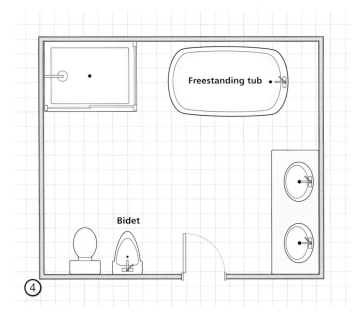

Freestanding tub

Bidet

④

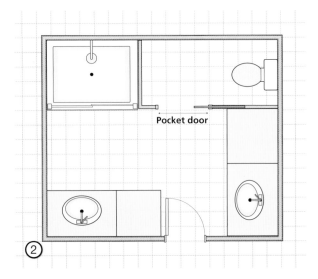

Pocket door

②

Half wall

⑤

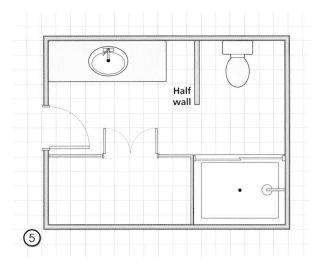

③

① This master bath includes a multi-head shower, double sinks, and a generous closet.

② The layout of this master bath is divided into purpose zones. Pocket doors separate the toilet from the rest of the room and provide two separate dressing areas.

③ Setting the fixtures against the walls of this narrow room leaves plenty of open space for users to enjoy.

④ This layout has it all: a commodious freestanding tub, large shower, double sinks, a toilet, and bidet.

⑤ A half wall between the toilet and vanity areas offers a degree of privacy without encroaching too much on the available space.

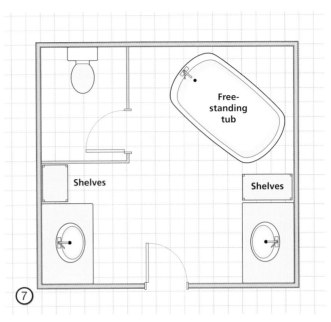

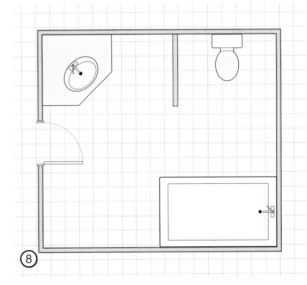

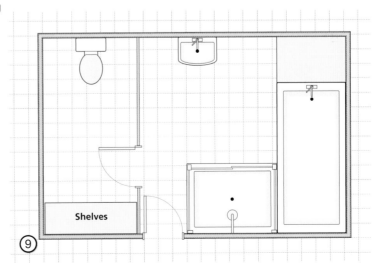

⑥ A partial wall houses plumbing lines and creates a sense of division between this small bathroom and the bedroom beyond.

⑦ Each vanity area has its own tower of shelves in this large layout. Setting a bathtub at an angle in a corner uses a lot of space, but can create a gracious atmosphere.

⑧ This layout leaves plenty of room to add freestanding furniture, which is extremely popular right now. With an open layout like this, you're free to add shelf and display units, and even chairs or benches.

⑨ The end of the large toilet area in this layout includes floor-to-ceiling shelves. The area around the sink is left open for freestanding display or shelf units.

Bathroom Styles

Trend watchers tell us the average bathroom has doubled in size since the 1970s. As the space devoted to baths has grown, so has our interest in bathroom style. We want to spend more time there: they are no longer spaces for washing, but places to relax and unwind. It's no longer enough to choose a matched set of fixtures and fittings. Today's homeowners want their bathrooms to have genuine style, as well as practical qualities.

But what exactly is style? Dictionary definitions of style include phrases such as *impressive flair* and *the state of being popular*. These definitions demonstrate the highly subjective nature of style, its elusive quality. Fortunately, it's easier to create style than to define it. You can either choose one style, such as minimalism, and reflect it in every element of the room, or mix and match traditional designs with minimalist or contemporary styles for an eclectic look. Like any other space in the house, it's the details that take a bathroom from nice to fabulous. From the flooring to the fittings and fixtures, from the light fixtures to the outlet covers, make sure each piece contributes to the whole.

With rare exception, bathrooms take their style cues from the rest of the house. It would be just as unlikely to find a Victorian bath in an extremely contemporary home as to find a stark minimalist bath in a historical restoration. Using the style of your home as a basis, the goal is to create the best possible representation of that style in the bathroom.

As though that weren't enough of a challenge, you must also consider the particular bathroom you're designing and the goals you have in mind for it. The choices you'd make for, let's say, a master bath might be quite different from the ones you'd make for a bathroom used primarily by children. A bath where you plan to linger and relax should be outfitted differently than one where speed and efficiency is the main concern.

In this chapter we'll take a look at several bathroom styles: minimalist, contemporary, period, and traditional. We'll also show you examples of these styles in bathrooms of a variety of types: master, family, and guest baths.

Take note of the details throughout. Colors, materials, and finishes help define a style, and certain themes are repeated. For instance, the glossy, brightly colored surfaces common in contemporary baths are rarely found in minimalist designs. Black works in almost any style, but isn't found very often in family or children's baths. Bear these details in mind as you establish the style of your bathroom.

Opposite: The subtle shapes and styles of these fixtures and fittings provide the perfect balance for a large Gothic window and folding screens in this traditional bathroom.

Below: In a minimalist bath, luxury is present without calling undue attention to itself. Great light, streamlined surfaces, and a black-and-white color scheme work together to create a stylish space.

Minimalist

Minimalist designs reduce a subject to its essential elements. Designer Buckminster Fuller once referred to minimalism as the effort to "do more with less." This is accomplished by paying special attention to the connection of lines and planes, the play of light, and the use of open space.

Every element of a minimalist bathroom is designed to meet its purpose as simply as possible. Bathrooms of this style offer all the features and comforts of more elaborate styles, but they accomplish it without unnecessary ornamentation or flourishes.

Minimalist design is heavily influenced by traditional Japanese design and architecture. Colors are often limited to black, white, and a range of neutrals.

① The unusually large floor tiles here echo the size and shape of the windows, reducing the number of lines competing for attention.

② Stainless steel and white dominate this streamlined bathroom, where shallow sinks are suspended on a wall of the same proportions.

③ Using a single color for the walls and floors, as shown here, visually erases a room's boundaries, creating an illusion of more space.

④ More and more often, homebuyers are requesting lounging space in bathrooms. This can be achieved without sacrificing minimal design, by adding just the right chair.

⑤ This elegant room proves that color and minimalism are not mutually exclusive. The red rectangle focuses the eye on the vanity wall and creates a sense of depth for the room.

⑥ The pedestal tub and vessel sink meld with the marble walls and floor in this sleek room.

Contemporary

Contemporary design strives to combine art with engineering. Its simple and sometimes highly stylized forms emphasize geometry, shape, and form. Bathrooms designed in this style incorporate the latest materials in a variety of colors.

The word contemporary means "characteristic of the present," but that does not equate to following short-lived trends. The goal is to create a room that looks modern not only today, but well into the future. That means skipping obvious trends and resisting high-concept pieces that may look dated by next year.

In these days of increasing concern about the environment, contemporary designers lead the trend toward practical, durable pieces that can be reused or recycled.

① Strong shapes play well against natural textures. Here, the simple lines of the fixtures contrast with the stone wall, wood vanity, and tub deck.

② Contemporary designers often add a traditional element for contrast, as with this chandelier.

③ Reminiscent of African drums, these sinks double as art.

④ Straight lines, a limited color palette, and an emphasis on symmetry give this large bathroom a contemporary feel.

⑤ The smooth white surfaces and geometric shapes of these fixtures offer an elegant contrast to the recycled bricks and wood floor.

⑥ The strong lines and deep color of this trough-like tub and sink define this room.

⑦ Metallic surfaces are common in contemporary design. Here, stainless steel teams with deep purple to create an elegant room.

⑤

⑥

⑦

Period and Traditional

Period and traditional styles include designs based on the experience of a historic era. The term "period" often refers to designs that reflect a specific point in time, such as the 18th century or even the 1950s. Traditional style typically refers to a formal style, such as Georgian, Victorian, or Arts and Crafts.

Although the look may come from the past, recreating the style of a particular era comes and goes with fashion—for instance, the early 21st century saw many bathrooms being decorated in the classic pinks and aquas popular in the 1950s. Period designs are faithful to the colors, textures, and shapes of the era being evoked. When designing a period room, researching the era can be a large part of the fun.

Traditional designs are often formal, and include symmetry, classic lines, and dark wood. Common colors include medium shades of blue, green, and rose with neutral or gold accents. Tone-on-tone, prints, and simple stripes are popular in traditional rooms.

① Rich plank flooring and decorative paint provide an Arts and Crafts-style background for a stunning bathtub.

② Black and chrome form the foundation of this Art Deco bathroom. The upholstered Lucite chair in the foreground is a treasure in a room like this.

③ This bathroom captures the elegance of the French Revolution era. Many retailers sell period paint colors and wallpaper for authentic interiors.

④ The robin's-egg blue tub and deeper blue floor give a nod to the Victorian era. The high-tank toilet is a reproduction.

⑤ Cabinets with the appearance of fine furniture, such as this elegant storage unit, tend to mesh well with the more formal furnishings of traditional-style homes.

⑥ A stylized pedestal sink and toilet enhance this traditional bath. Before you buy a toilet with an unusual shape, such as this, make sure it's comfortable for you.

Master Bathrooms

A "master bathroom" (a bath adjoining the home's main bedroom) has become a virtual necessity in today's market. Adding a master bath is a home improvement that will repay you by increasing your home's dollar value and its attractiveness to buyers.

Designing a master bath that successfully serves two people requires good communication. Couples need to talk about how their habits and preferences affect the best layout for their bathroom. For example, partners who value privacy would be well served by a bathroom with some type of separation between the bathing, toilet, and vanity areas. Others might prefer the togetherness of a large, multi-head shower, or the luxury of an oversized bathtub or whirlpool. Couples who have different schedules may prefer to separate the bathroom from the bedroom by a door.

① An oversized tub is a welcome addition to many master baths. This model is deep enough for a good soaking and includes a handheld shower.

② A vanity, open shower, and soaking tub are in an alcove in this master bedroom.

③ Even small bathrooms can be luxurious. A trough-like, deep tub provides maximum room for soaking in a minimal space.

④ Details such as individual robe hooks, towel bars, and double sinks make a big difference when two people are getting ready at the same time.

⑤ An abundance of natural light and open space make this master bath a pleasure to share, especially on chilly mornings when the fire is lit.

⑥ This master bath enjoys the true luxury of wide-open spaces. With a wall-mounted vanity and compact linen cabinet tucked against the wall, the center of the room offers space to bathe or simply relax.

Family Bathrooms

Designed to be shared by several people, family baths are dedicated to efficiency. That doesn't mean they can't be stylish, only that their function demands durable, low-maintenance fixtures and materials.

Adequate storage is critical to successful family baths. They need plenty of cabinets and drawers for toiletries and towels, as well as a laundry hamper or other designated place to stash wet towels and dirty laundry.

Small children need less help in the bathroom if they can reach the sink themselves. Consider building a stepstool into a cabinet toe kick to help them become more self-sufficient. And remember to include at least one locking cabinet so you can keep medicines and other hazardous materials out of their reach.

① A whole family could easily get ready in this spacious bath. One side of the partition wall supports the sink; the other provides storage and offers privacy for bathers.

② Two sinks, four shelves, lots of cabinets, and a niche for extra toilet paper all add up to a successful family bath.

③ Adequate storage is critical in family baths, where several people need space for their toiletries and supplies. This bathroom makes good use of ledges and open shelves as well as multiple drawers in the vanity.

④ Durable materials are essential for a family bathroom. Here, tile protects the walls and floors, while textured enamel cabinets repel fingerprints.

⑤ Handheld showers help children wash their own hair or take a shower on their own.

⑥ Placing cabinets within reach lets little ones put away their toys and dirty clothes when bath time is over.

Guest Bathrooms

Simple comfort and convenience drive the decisions about guest baths. Unlike master baths, where luxury can be a key element, guest baths are more about function. Guests need to shower and dress, but they're unlikely to need whirlpool tubs or shower towers.

Guest baths are typically smaller and used less frequently than master or family baths. These factors provide opportunities to use materials that might be too expensive in a large bath or impractical in a heavily used bath. This might be the place for that gorgeous foil wallpaper you love or the glass vessel sink you've had your eye on.

Feel free to use cabinets and drawers to store household items, but leave at least one shelf and one drawer empty for the convenience of your guests.

① Glass shelves, a shower caddy, and a towel stand keep the necessities accessible in this cheery guest bath.

② While it might be expensive to use glass tile in a larger bath, this bathroom's smaller scale makes it affordable.

③ A towel warmer is a nice touch for guests. Open shelves, such as the ones under this sink, work well, too. Keep towels and other necessities in sight and within easy reach so guests don't have to hunt for them.

④ A streamlined toilet and wall-hung vanity create extra space in this small but welcoming room.

⑤ A limited amount of space does not have to mean sacrificing style or facilities, as shown here. A deep window well holds a stack of towels within easy reach of both the sink and shower.

⑥ In addition to the wall-hung vanity and cabinet, an alcove wall cut-out gives guests plenty of space to store toiletries and cosmetics during their visit.

Bathtubs

There are quicker, more efficient ways to get clean, but for many people efficiency is no substitute for the marvelous comfort of a long, hot bath. Luxurious bathing starts with the bathtub itself, and choosing the right one is not a matter of chance. Rather, it's a matter of matching the size, shape, and features of the tub to the people who will use it as well as to the room where it will be installed.

B athtubs have been popular for thousands of years. Archeologists have discovered individual-sized bathtubs in palaces and ordinary homes from India to the island of Crete. The materials are different and today's technology has led to additional amenities, but modern tubs are amazingly similar to the ones unearthed in ancient homes.

No matter what its shape or how it's accessorized, a bathtub is a watertight vessel with access to the home's plumbing system and its drain/waste/vent system. Beyond those basics, virtually anything goes, from aromatherapy or chromatherapy to air jets and multimedia.

With a world of choices before you, how do you select a bathtub? Start with the space available: the bathtub has to fit the room *and* leave space for other fixtures and activities. The layout of the room will, to a large extent, dictate the size and type—alcove, freestanding, built-in—of tub you choose.

Next, consider who will use the tub and how the tub will be used. Soaking in hot water up to your chin requires a different type of tub than bathing several children. And it goes without saying that a six-foot person probably won't be comfortable in a tub made for someone who's much shorter.

After you've assessed the space available and evaluated how the tub will be used, you're ready to shop. It's time to click through websites and wander through showrooms, stopping along the way to learn about features and materials, too. When you find a model that seems to suit your needs, test-drive it in real life. You might feel a little silly crawling into a bathtub in a showroom, but that doesn't compare to how you'll feel after it's installed if you discover you just can't get comfortable or that leaning against the backrest puts a crick in your neck.

This chapter is filled with bathtubs of all types—freestanding, built-in, and sunken. In these pages, you'll learn the differences between claw foot and pedestal tubs, alcoves and built-ins, whirlpools and air jets, and you'll see examples of the latest tub technology.

Opposite: A backdrop of natural greenery here enhances the experience that only bathtubs can provide.

Below: Here's a stunning traditional bathtub with a modern twist: shower fittings, including a rain shower, directly overhead.

Types, Sizes, and Styles

We've come a long way since bathtubs were little more than horse troughs lined with porcelain. Today, bathtubs are manufactured in nearly every shape and size imaginable. Standard tubs start at 30 x 60 inches (75 x 150 cm) to as large as 36 x 72 inches (90 x 180 cm). Whirlpool baths can be 60 x 60 inches (150 x 150 cm) or larger.

Make sure the tub you select works with the floor plan of your bathroom and the way you live. It is also important to take basic structural matters into consideration when selecting a bathtub. A sunken tub may not be a practical choice for a remodeling project in a ranch home built on a concrete slab. Large cast-iron or stone tubs sometimes require additional support for the floor, which also can be challenging in remodeling projects.

① This stone tub is set into a custom-built surround. The deep oval design is perfect for soaking in.

② "Infinity tubs" like this take a two-tiered approach to bathing. There are drains in the outer tub designed to handle displaced water from the main tub as well as water from the hand-held shower.

③ The hourglass shape of this sunken whirlpool slightly reduces the amount of water required to fill it without reducing its comfort.

④ This sleek oval, served by a hand-held shower, cradles bathers in a molded backrest.

⑤ A rich wood apron adds texture and interest to this rectangular tub. Although it could sit in an alcove, this tub is finished on three sides.

①

②

Materials

A bathtub's material affects its appearance and shape as well as its durability and, most especially, its price. Each material has advantages and disadvantages. Some, like fiberglass, tend to be inexpensive and lightweight, but may not be as durable as you'd like. Others, such as wood and metal, offer high style and natural beauty, but may be quite expensive and sometimes require a substantial commitment to maintenance.

One of the most important characteristics of a bathtub material is its weight. Extremely heavy tubs, such as large stone or cast-iron models, may require that the floors of the bathroom be reinforced to bear the load. Be sure to verify the structural requirements of these tubs before purchase.

① The nickel lining of this bathtub contrasts beautifully with its copper exterior. Typically, tubs like this are handmade and may include visible seams.

② Enameled steel is less expensive and lighter than cast iron, but may not hold heat well and can be noisy. Some high-quality versions have an undercoating that helps resolve these issues.

③ This freestanding stone tub is simply stunning. Stone bathtubs are extremely durable, but tend to be heavy and expensive. Still, there's nothing in the world quite like the natural beauty of stone.

④ Glass and stainless steel combine to create an almost magical bathtub here. The glass itself is manufactured for safety. Some manufacturers add a spot-resistant coating.

⑤ And now for the *truly* exotic: an acrylic bathtub wrapped in crocodile leather. Acrylic tubs tend to be lightweight, durable, and resistant to scratches. And the crocodile leather? Well, that's already proven itself around water, hasn't it?

⑥ Special finishes can make wood tubs last for generations. Most require a commitment to occasional maintenance, but this is a small price to pay for those who love the grain and substance of wood.

Freestanding Tubs

The cycle of fashion means that everything old is thought to be new again, eventually. So it is with freestanding tubs. During the mid-1800s, the bathtub in virtually every home was a freestanding vessel. By the mid-1900s, the trend toward built-in tubs swept the countryside, and hundreds of thousands of freestanding tubs were cast aside. In recent years, they have become fashionable again, and now many buyers are willing to pay a premium for the elegance and romance of a freestanding tub.

Today's freestanding tub isn't exactly the same as the one grandma used to have, though. The new versions are made of materials ranging from the old favorite, cast iron, to porcelain on steel, acrylic, stone, metal—even glass. Some have jets and some have colored lights. Take a look at what's happening now.

① A wood surround warms this gleaming white pedestal tub. A wooden pillar beside the tub provides subtle housing for the faucet, spout, and hand-held showerhead.

② Balls support this traditional freestanding tub, creating an interesting and unique design.

③ A wooden brace cradles this rolled-edge tub. Note the convenient towel rack suspended beneath the tub's edge.

④ This freestanding tub sits in front of a freestanding wall, anchoring it in the center of the room.

⑤ This glorious copper tub rests on a wood pedestal. A tall, goose-necked faucet delivers water to the tub, matching the style of the faucets behind the sinks.

⑥ With its polished wood legs and chrome rail, this tub has a flair for the dramatic. It fits in well with the romance of the marble and chandelier.

Continued from page 34.

Freestanding tubs have a number of advantages. They're easy to install, simple to maintain, and add a touch of elegance to a bathroom. Installation is easy because, by definition, there's no framing involved—the tub isn't being set into anything. Maintenance is simple because the drains and other plumbing elements are readily accessible, especially on traditional American designs, which feature tub-mounted hardware. (Traditional European designs feature wall-mounted hardware.)

Claw-foot tubs are typically ovals with rolled edges. Some sort of feet, often metal, support the tubs themselves. Slipper tubs, variations of traditional claw-foot tubs, slope upward at one end to provide support for the bather's back.

Pedestal tubs are supported by bases rather than legs. These bases are often wood, but may be made of any material that will support the weight of the loaded tub.

Soaking tubs can be any size or shape. They're designed to rest directly on the floor.

① Basic soaking tub, finished on all sides
② Traditional claw-foot tub with tub-mounted hardware
③ Contemporary soaking tub featuring wooden end caps
④ Oval tub supported by stylized mahogany legs
⑤ Slipper tub with elegant brass feet
⑥ Compact pedestal tub with built-in backrest
⑦ Modern claw-foot tub encased in a gleaming chrome support system
⑧ Freestanding round tub set into a square wood surround
⑨ Contemporary oval soaking tub with jets
⑩ Infinity soaking tub (surrounded by a channel that drains overflow into the drain/waste/vent system)
⑪ Round, Japanese-style pedestal tub
⑫ Contemporary rectangular soaking tub with surface-mounted hardware

(5)

(9)

(6)

(10)

(7)

(11)

(8)

(12)

Built-in Tubs

In the mid-1900s, homebuilders began to introduce built-in bathtubs into homes. They quickly surpassed freestanding tubs in popularity. In fact, they are the most common types of bathtubs in modern homes. The reasons are hardly mysterious: they're less expensive than comparable freestanding tubs and use space efficiently.

Built-in tubs cost less than similar freestanding models because they're finished only on the sides that show. For example, only the front or *apron* of an alcove tub needs to be finished. Contrast that with the 360° finish of a freestanding tub and it's easy to see why the built-in costs are lower.

Built-in tubs are especially useful in bathrooms where space is at a premium. Because they rest against at least one wall, it takes fewer square feet to meet the guidelines for access standards and create efficient traffic patterns.

① This drop-in tub is finished on three sides. The wooden steps and deck surrounding it offer an interesting design element as well as providing seating.

② Vivid red accents liven up a simple drop-in tub in this contemporary bathroom. Imagination has been used in adding extra features that produce dazzling results.

③ An oval drop-in tub within a rectangular surround enhances the effect of the oval sinks on the narrow counter. Extending the tile across the entire arrangement makes it appear to be one piece.

④ Tiled steps lead to this tub that has been built into a spacious deck surrounded by windows, creating a very elegant layout.

⑤ More interesting than a standard rectangular tub, this model includes a finished apron on the rounded front. The floor of this tub is rectangular, but the elongated sides make it appear to smile.

⑥ This oval drop-in includes grab bars that make it easier for bathers to get into and out of the tub.

⑦ Set against a wide window, bathing in this drop-in tub would be like floating in a sea of tranquility.

Alcove tubs are surrounded by walls on three sides. This makes it particularly easy to install convenient grab bars and rails. Manufacturers recognize the importance of this issue. Many even offer alcove units with doors so bathers can walk in rather than step over the edge of the tub.

Alcove tubs typically are served by wall-mounted faucets and have drains at the end nearest those faucets. Units with only one apron are sold as "left hand" or "right hand" models, depending on the location of the predrilled holes for the drain and overflow. Many alcove tubs are tub and shower combinations that include molded surround walls.

Drop-in tubs are set into raised platforms or *decks*. Some have steps leading to them in order to make it easier for bathers to get in and out. They typically are designed for tub-mounted faucets. They are rarely available in tub and shower combinations because they are not enclosed.

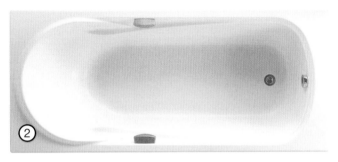

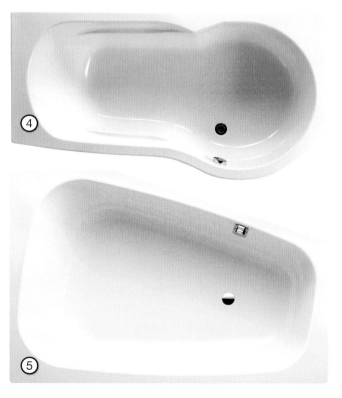

① Drop-in tub with centered drain and grab bar
② Right-hand alcove tub with molded backrest and grab bars
③ Simple drop-in with centered drain and overflow
④ Acrylic, keyhole-shaped drop-in with off-center drain and overflow
⑤ Angled drop-in with right-hand drain and overflow
⑥ Left-hand alcove with molded head rest and grab bars
⑦ Acrylic right-hand alcove with built-in grab bars
⑧ Drop-in with built-in grab bars
⑨ Right-hand alcove with grab bars; designed for one bather
⑩ Acrylic rounded alcove with built-in shelf
⑪ Left-hand alcove with generous proportions
⑫ Left-hand drop-in; designed for two bathers
⑬ Oval drop-in with centered drain and overflow
⑭ Corner drop-in with centered drain and built-in ledge

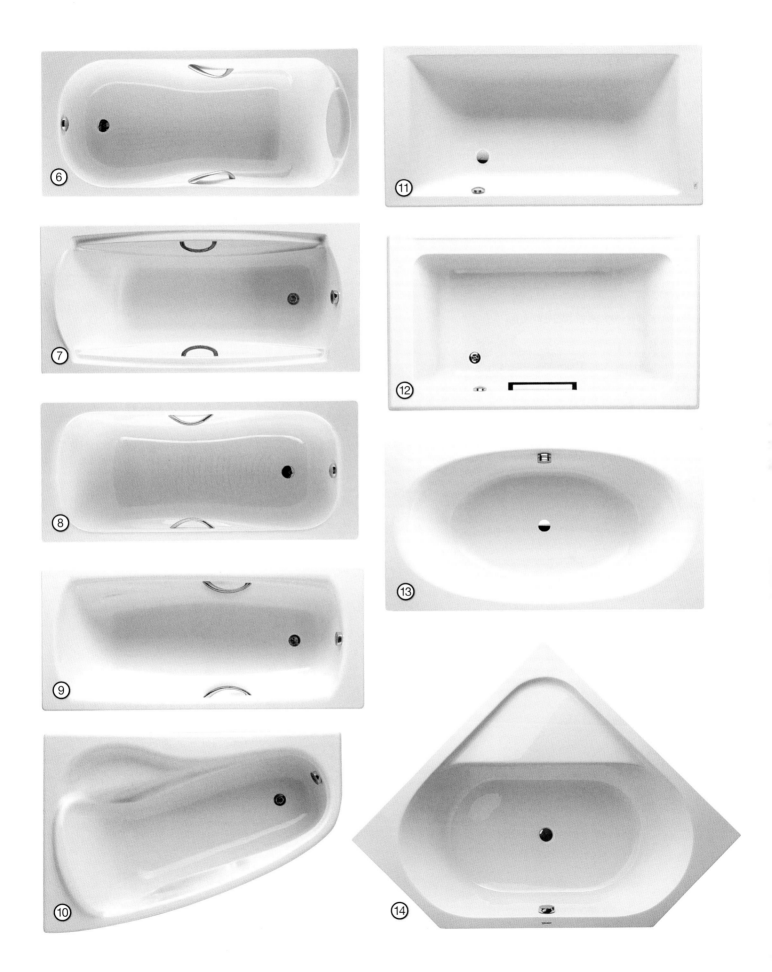

Sunken Tubs

Sunken tubs are glamorous—they conjure up images of princesses, movie stars, and romantic adventures. In the right situation, a sunken tub can transform an average bathroom into an elegant retreat.

Make sure you have plenty of space in the bathroom and money in the budget before you set your heart on a sunken tub. Installing one requires careful planning, and the services of an architect may be necessary. Making sure the tub is properly supported requires specialized skills that not all contractors possess.

One note of caution: be very careful about where you install a sunken tub. In homes with children or elderly family members, they can lead to accidents. Even if your home includes only healthy adults, always leave a light burning in a bathroom with a sunken tub.

① The gleaming white whirlpool tub sunk into the floor transforms this sumptuous bathroom into a personal spa.

② Grab bars, such as the ones built into this oversized whirlpool tub, make it easier and safer to get in and out of a sunken tub.

③ Shoji screens protect this sunken whirlpool tub, creating an atmosphere dedicated to relaxation.

④ An acrylic tub sunk into a tiled alcove offers a private retreat here.

⑤ A custom-built tiled tub awaits lucky bathers in this simple but gracious bathroom.

⑥ Slatted wood floors surround this sunken tub, giving the bathroom an earthy, natural feel.

Whirlpool and Spa Tubs

Whirlpools and spas are enjoying a resurgence
these days. In the 1980s, a whirlpool tub or spa
was practically mandatory for a well-appointed
bathroom. Then, in the 1990s and early 2000s,
the pendulum swung, and people began to realize
they rarely used them. It took too much hot water
to fill them and there were concerns about the
growth of bacteria in the lines.

Today, new technology and maintenance
methods have cleared up those safety concerns.
Highly efficient, tankless water heaters provide
an endless supply of hot water. In short, there's
no longer any reason to miss out on the health
benefits and pleasure of owning a whirlpool or spa.

The maintenance requirements of whirlpool tubs
vary widely. When shopping for one, ask questions
about the maintenance required to keep the unit
free of bacteria. In response to health concerns,
manufacturers have created new technology,
including air jets. Air jets circulate warm air rather
than water, which eliminates the possibility of
stagnant, bacteria-prone water in the lines.

① Air-jet tubs circulate warm air that produces bubbles in
the bath.

② Molded accessories, such as the seat at the side of
this oval whirlpool, are designed to make tubs more
convenient and comfortable.

③ This round, freestanding tub accommodates two bathers
in very little more space than a standard tub. Built-in
seats are the secrets to its success.

④ A freestanding whirlpool gives you easy access to all of
the working parts. This acrylic-and-wood model offers
style and great comfort.

Tub Technology

Bathtubs are no longer static vessels filled with water, or even whirlpool jets. Today's tubs circulate the water, keep it warm, and use it to massage specific areas of the body. If that doesn't satisfy you, today's tubs can also soothe you with music, colored lights, and aromatherapy.

Tub technology now incorporates music therapy (the use of music to elevate the emotions), chromatherapy (the use of colors to stimulate healing), and aromatherapy (which uses aromatic oils to calm or stimulate the nervous system). Opinions may be divided on the healing benefits of these therapies, but it's hard to dispute the pleasure they add to the bathing experience.

① This tub starts with a whirlpool, adds a foot, neck, and lumbar massage system, and then tops it off with a CD/radio player—all controlled through a digital touch-screen panel.

② Lights in the side panels of this soaking tub create the illusion of bathing in a pool of flowing pink light.

③ Set the light to suit your mood in this tub. Here, the lights simulate the glow of candlelight.

④ A slight adjustment produces the golden glow of a sunset on demand.

⑤ If you want to, you can start the day with an energizing burst of pink light.

⑥ Calm yourself with serene blue water, like the water here, whenever you choose!

Showers and Wet Rooms

Elaborate, multi-head showers are one of the hottest trends in bathroom design these days. People who find themselves in too much of a hurry to fill a whirlpool tub, let alone soak in it, still want to start and end their days in luxury. And that's what today's showers deliver: thermostatic controls, pulsating, massaging jets aimed at the whole body, maybe even some soothing light or aromatherapy.

Although the trend toward showers is a strong one, not just any shower will do. Today's showers are luxurious affairs with showerheads that deliver flows resembling everything from gentle rain to pummeling waterfalls. Head-to-toe body jets massage away aches and pains, and steam units envelop you in warmth and fragrance.

Not everyone has the space or budget for these amenities, but that doesn't mean they can't create a shower with a spa-like atmosphere, one that gives them a place to relax and pamper themselves. In today's market, there are exceptionally fine shower products designed to fit virtually every space and budget. With complex shower towers on one end of the scale and simple rainhead showers on the other, there really is something for everyone.

Practically unheard of a decade or so ago, the term "wet room" refers to another of the major trends in bathroom design. Wet rooms are designed so that the entire space can be exposed to water: walls, floors, and even ceilings are covered with waterproof materials. Showers are not separated from the rest of the room by walls or other dividers and centrally located drains carry away water from showers and other bathing activities. Wet rooms can easily be designed to be barrier-free—a dream when it comes to accessibility.

As you read through this chapter, consider what type of shower experience you're seeking and what components are necessary to provide that performance. As you look at the examples shown here, take notes on the showers that appeal to you, the types of spray you like, and the direction or directions water can come from. This type of information will be invaluable when you sit down with a designer or contractor to plan a bathroom project and again when you begin shopping for shower components.

Opposite: With a rainhead suspended from the ceiling and a handheld shower extending from the wall, this glass-enclosed shower is as practical as it is beautiful.

Below: If you've dreamed of bathing beneath a waterfall, perhaps this is the shower for you.

Types, Sizes, and Styles

The recent emphasis on showers and showerheads has led to an explosion in the types of showers available.

Prefab showers are stock enclosures, most often made of glass, fiberglass, or acrylic.

Custom enclosures are designed especially for a bathroom, and can accommodate any configuration of showerheads and fittings you like.

Shower towers are special units containing electric pumps that enhance the water pressure as well as its temperature.

Shower/bath combinations, once the standard when it comes to showers, are still incredibly popular. They are created by adding shower fittings to a bathtub.

Steam showers are shower units that include a steam generator as well as one or more showerheads.

Wet rooms are completely open, including the shower area. Every aspect of a wet room must be watertight, which makes them rather expensive to build.

③

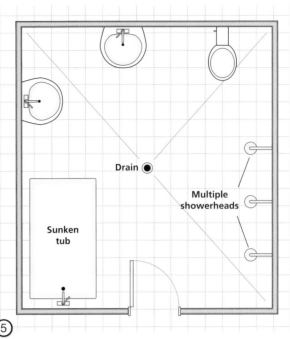

④

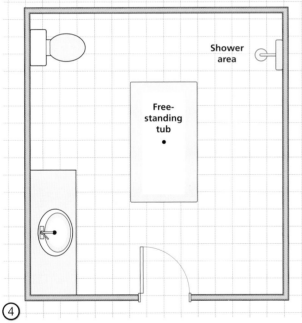

⑤

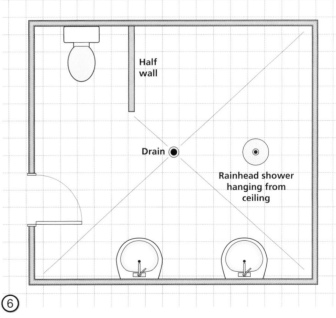

⑥

① A glass panel protects the rest of the bathroom from the spray in this modified open shower.

② An adjustable-height showerhead is particularly appropriate for family and children's baths, where the heights of the users may vary widely.

③ This bathroom design features a sunken tub, corner shower, and enclosed toilet area. It also encompasses the master closet, an arrangement that greatly simplifies the process of dressing.

④ This open shower blends into the background, allowing the freestanding tub to take center stage.

⑤ The design for this wet room features multiple showerheads in the shower area, a sunken tub, and dual sinks as well as a wall-hung toilet.

⑥ This wet room design brings practically the entire room into the shower. A half wall separates the toilet area, leaving the room completely accessible and easy to use.

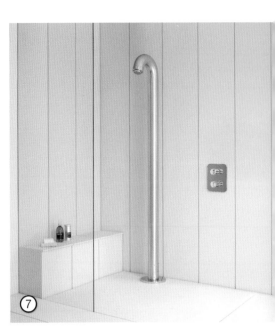

① Chrome arms hold a glass panel in position to contain the shower spray in this ceramic tile enclosure.

② The action of a rainhead shower feels wonderful, but its positioning means your hair always gets wet when using it. A supplemental handheld shower lets users clean up without washing their hair.

③ Set in a white room, with full-glass enclosure and white shower tray, this shower looks as if it is floating.

④ Angled screens provide privacy for this spacious walk-in shower. The column that supports the screens also houses the showerhead and controls.

⑤ Glass panels and double doors enclose this shower. The drain in this shower tray is out of the ordinary—a slit rather than the typical circle.

⑥ This custom-built tile shower encompasses several windows (and window ledges) as well as a seat. Most users appreciate ledges and shelves in a shower, and seats are among the most requested shower amenities.

⑦ The vertical lines in this wall treatment emphasize the unusual size and shape of this standpipe and showerhead.

Shower Enclosures

Shower enclosures come in two basic varieties. The right enclosure for your bathroom is one that combines the look you prefer with a size and shape that suits your room.

Framed enclosures are sturdy and economical. Most use lighter-weight glass than their frameless counterparts.

Frameless enclosures are very popular because their relative lack of hardware creates clean, elegant lines. However, they're more expensive than framed enclosures, mostly because they require thicker glass and special clips and hinges. They're also the most difficult to install, which translates to higher costs when you're hiring a contractor.

Remember: clear-glass enclosures are appealing in books, magazines, and catalogs, but every water spot shows on them. Patterned or frosted glass, which provides a bit of privacy, is easier to maintain.

① A glass shower enclosure showcases the flow of the intricate tile work from wall to shower to wall.

② A frameless glass door encloses this ceramic-tile shower. Notice how tiles in a darker shade have been used to create a simple but striking design for the end wall.

③ Two glass panels and a door enclose a small but attractive corner shower. A shower like this is easy for homeowners to install themselves.

④ The pure white walls and floor of this one-piece alcove shower are contrasted with black tile for a dramatic, custom-built appearance.

⑤ Frameless glass doors allow this shower to blend into the surrounding room with barely a ripple.

⑥ Graceful curves make this corner shower a real showstopper. Although most rainheads are suspended from the ceiling, this one is cleverly held in position by a chrome extender.

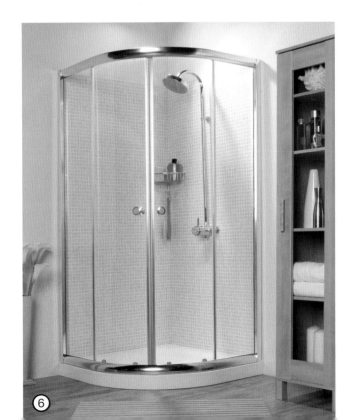

Another important characteristic of a shower enclosure is its shape.

D-shaped enclosures fit against one flat wall, curving away and back from the wall.

Quadrant enclosures fit into corners. Their sides may be curved or angled.

Square and rectangular enclosures can be used almost anywhere, and are frequently found in alcoves.

Walk-in enclosures typically consist of a large showering area shielded by a screen.

① Semi-circular quadrant enclosure with clear glass
② Framed quadrant enclosure
③ Round, quadrant enclosure
④ Frameless, clear-glass enclosure
⑤ Frameless enclosure with colored glass panel
⑥ Framed glass enclosure with frameless pivot door
⑦ Clear-glass panel and door
⑧ Square quadrant enclosure
⑨ Framed rectangular enclosure
⑩ Framed enclosure with adjacent drying area
⑪ Frameless enclosure suspended from top frame
⑫ Frameless walk-in enclosure
⑬ Pivot doors on a framed enclosure
⑭ Square-framed enclosure in corner setting
⑮ Frameless quadrant enclosure with clear glass
⑯ Curved quadrant enclosure
⑰ Clear glass suspended from top frame
⑱ Framed enclosure with colored glass and pivot door
⑲ Framed rectangular enclosure with pivot door
⑳ Rectangular shower with glass door

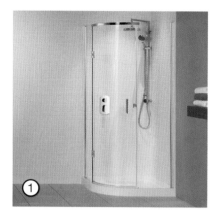

9

13

17

10

14

18

11

15

19

12

16

20

The right showerhead contributes greatly to the quality of a shower experience.

Handheld showers are connected to flexible hoses attached to fixed showerheads or the shower wall.

Multi-function showerheads offer a variety of spray patterns, from gentle mist to pulsating massage. They are adjusted by twisting the faceplate.

① Showerheads ranging from 4 to 24 inches (10 to 60 cm) in diameter
② Detachable handheld shower on adjustable bar
③ Massaging handheld shower connected to adjustable bar
④ Rain shower with extended riser
⑤ Contemporary showerhead on exposed riser with handheld accessory
⑥ Showerhead with pulse massage spray
⑦ Showerhead with full massage spray
⑧ Showerhead with champagne spray
⑨ Showerhead with needle or intense spray
⑩ Showerhead with focused massage spray
⑪ Showerhead with standard spray
⑫ Showerhead with aeration spray
⑬ Multi-function showerhead
⑭ Wide, oval showerhead
⑮ Multi-function showerhead with pulsating action
⑯ Multi-function showerhead with contemporary lines
⑰ Contemporary style, handheld shower attached to adjustable track

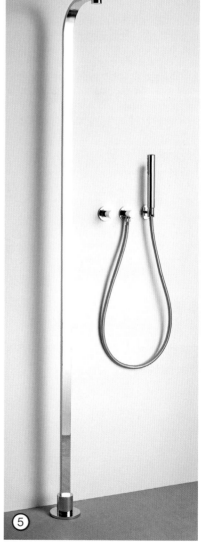

(6)

(10)

(14)

(7)

(11)

(15)

(8)

(12)

(16)

(9)

(13)

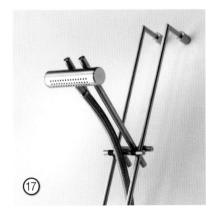

(17)

Rain showers are oversized showerheads installed directly overhead. They range from 5 to 16 inches (12 to 40 cm) in diameter. Most are suspended from the ceiling, but some are held in position by extended risers.

Waterfall showers are a variation on rain showers. Oversized and powerful, they deliver a streaming sheet of water, usually from directly overhead.

Multiple-head showers offer combinations of sizes, shapes, and spray patterns positioned at various heights to spray in a variety of directions. Many offer massaging or pulsating action. This design may require more substantial water pressure or larger supply pipes than typically found in today's bathrooms.

① Waterfall showerhead
② Sculptural version of a rainhead
③ Square rainhead
④ Round rainhead with vigorous action
⑤ Rectangular showerhead with two round sprays
⑥ Large brass rainhead
⑦ Square rainhead
⑧ Rainhead with adjustable spray
⑨ Multiple-head shower with body jets
⑩ Thin, contemporary rainhead
⑪ Large rainhead
⑫ Square rainhead with elaborate spray
⑬ Traditional-style rainhead
⑭ Pulsating body jet
⑮ Massage-action body jet
⑯ Vigorous spray body jet
⑰ Rainhead with adjustable sprays

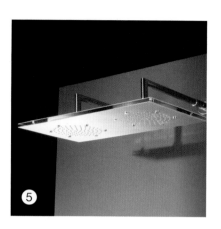

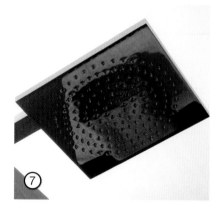

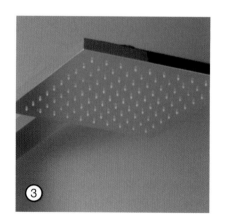

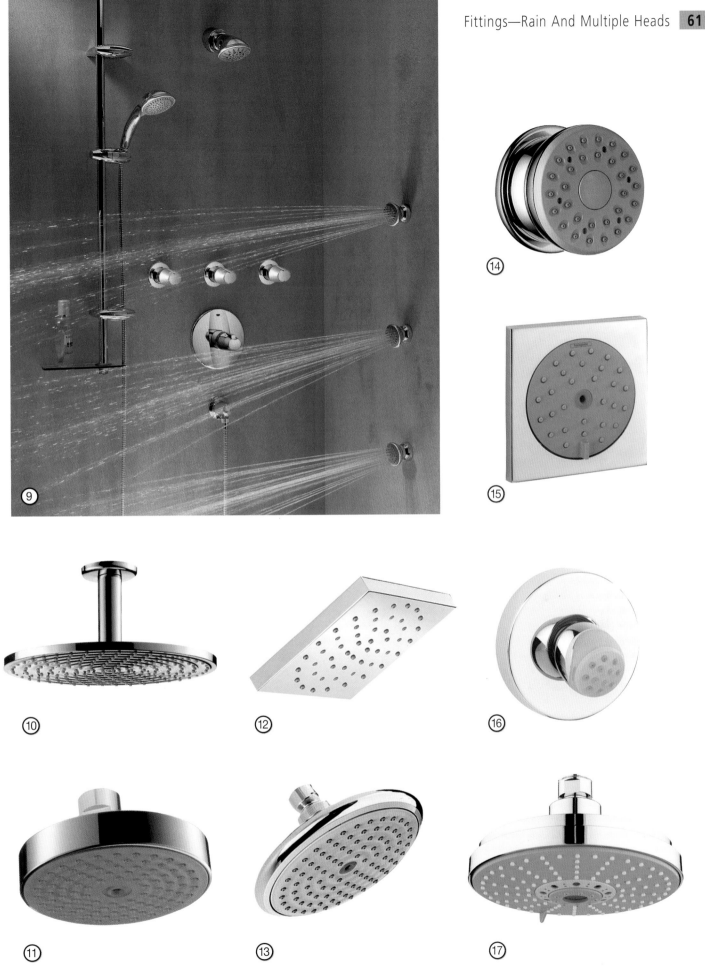

⑨

⑩

⑪

⑫

⑬

⑭

⑮

⑯

⑰

Shower controls have become more sophisticated in recent years, along with other aspects of today's showers.

Manual mixer valves mix hot and cold water to the comfort level of the user. They are economical and easy to use, but may leave users vulnerable to extremes in temperature when water is drawn from other parts of the house while the shower is in use.

Thermostatic mixers include hot and cold water supplies connected to a single valve complete with a built-in stabilizer that adjusts the temperature of the water. They maintain the temperature of the water, even if water is drawn elsewhere in the system.

① Push-button controls
② Dial control
③ Chrome controls
④ Contemporary, post-like controls
⑤ Ceramic handles on traditional-style controls
⑥ Multiple controls with buttons
⑦ Hot and cold control knobs
⑧ Multiple controls with adjustable thermostat
⑨ Individual control with adjustable thermostat
⑩ Single and double chrome controls
⑪ Thermostatic controls for body sprays and shower head
⑫ Single contemporary lever control
⑬ Contemporary-style, dual-handle controls
⑭ Single-handle chrome control
⑮ Round dual-handle controls

①

④

⑤

②

③

⑥

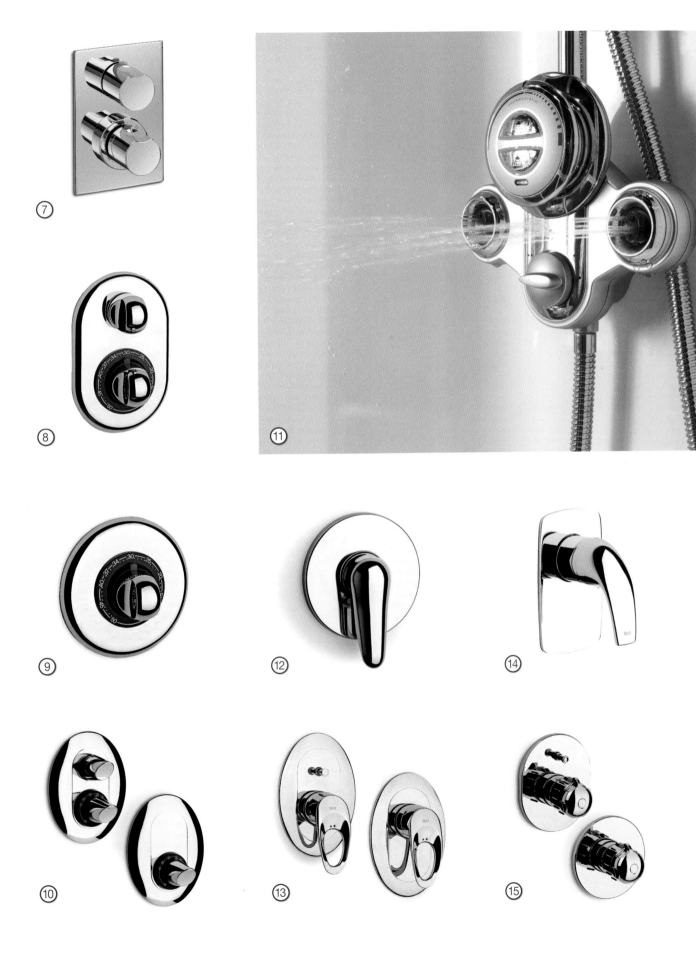

(7)

(8)

(9)

(10)

(11)

(12)

(13)

(14)

(15)

Shower Towers

Shower towers provide the ultimate in showering luxury. These multi-head units contain electric pumps that can increase both the pressure and temperature of the water. By pumping up the water pressure, they can produce exceptional massaging and pulsating action through a variety of showerheads and jets aimed at the whole body, from head to toe.

Shower towers require both cold and hot water supply lines, as they aren't meant to produce hot water, only to boost the temperature of warm water coming into the system. They also require adequate pressure coming into their system, usually at least 50psi, and sometimes demand larger than normal drains to handle the increased flow of water into the waste plumbing system.

① With body jets on both sides and a showerhead directly overhead, this shower provides massaging action from every direction.

② A shower tower provides plenty of action in this large, open shower.

③ This compact shower tower delivers excellent action in a small space.

④ This stylish unit is color-coordinated with the shower enclosure.

⑤ This unit includes a handheld shower, overhead spray, and six body jets.

④

③

⑤

Shower towers are available in a number of finishes as well as sizes and configurations. The best one for your bathroom depends on the size of the shower itself as well as the number of people likely to use the shower at one time. Larger showers meant for multiple users are best suited to units with larger numbers of sprays and jets. Conversely, smaller showers and single users may be overpowered by too many sprays.

Shower towers also vary in appearance, though most are rather modern-looking. Finishes range from chrome to brushed stainless steel to wood grain.

① Streamlined unit with height-adjustable rainhead and multiple body sprays
② Smaller unit with adjustable showerhead and fixed central spray
③ Shower arch fitted with body sprays, overhead spray, and handheld shower
④ Small, contemporary unit with fixed sprays as well as handheld shower
⑤ Shower tower with multiple body jets
⑥ Tower with adjustable-height handheld shower, body jets, and two shelves
⑦ Elaborate unit with fixed overhead shower, handheld shower, and multiple body jets
⑧ Stainless-steel unit with multiple showerheads, built-in shelf, and fog-free mirror
⑨ Stainless-steel and wood-grained tower with fixed and handheld shower, plus four body jets and an attached shelf
⑩ Translucent panel with overhead and handheld shower as well as multiple body jets
⑪ Wood-grain tower with rain and handheld shower and six body jets

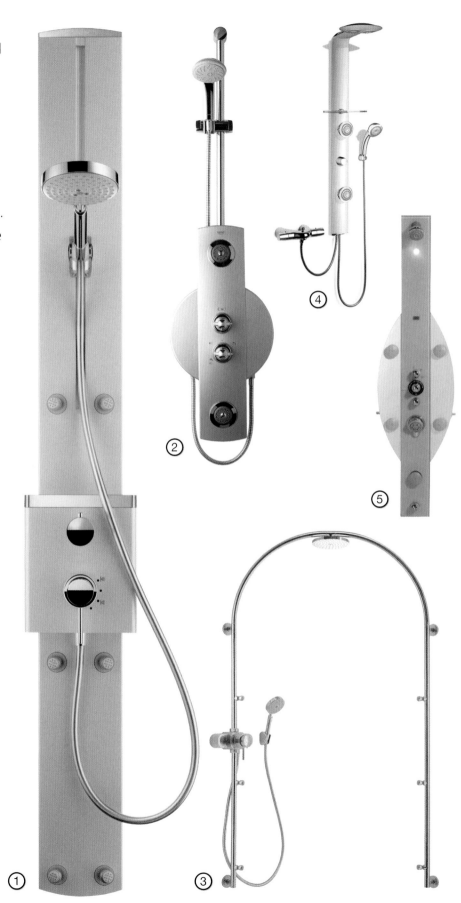

Shower/Bath Combinations

Shower/bath combinations are popular because they serve two purposes in one space. They're practical, attractive, and most are economical as well.

Shower/bath combinations involve a tub, enclosure, and both tub and shower spouts and fittings. Although some include full glass doors, others have glass shields or remain open to accommodate shower curtains. The walls of a shower/bath combination must be made of water-resistant materials, such as tile, solid-surface materials, acrylic, or fiberglass.

Some combinations are custom built, starting with a bathtub and tiled walls. Others are prefabricated one- or two-piece units that provide both the tub and water-resistant wall surfaces. When choosing a one-piece prefab unit for a remodeling project, make sure you can actually get the unit into the bathroom. Large models may not fit through the doorways.

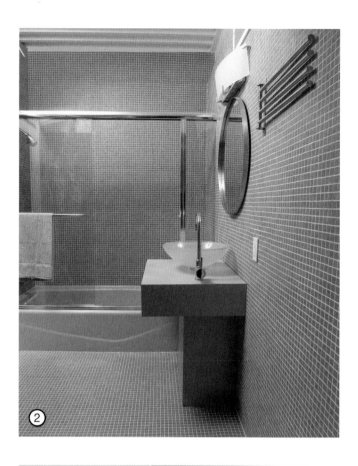

②

①

③

① A handheld showerhead serves this tub/shower combination. A glass panel shields the room from splashes, and wall niches provide storage space.

② This shower/tub alcove is enclosed by sliding glass doors.

③ A colorful panel, coordinated with the tile floor, shields the splash zone at the head of this shower/bath combination.

④ An extra-deep soaking tub is fitted with a clear-glass splash panel and a handheld shower.

⑤ A curved shower/bath combination, complete with clear-glass panel, fits into a tiled corner of this bathroom.

⑥ A tiled alcove and drop-in tub surrounded by framed pivoting doors creates generous, attractive space for this shower/bath.

Fittings for shower/bath combinations are usually sold with a "full combination" of components, which includes the basic valve, tub filler spout, showerhead, shower arm flange, and diverter provision. The tube waste and overflow assemblies are sold separately.

① Chrome spout, handles fitted to the side of the tub, and a frame supporting an overhead rain shower

② Standard wall-mounted showerhead over a deep soaking tub

③ Wall-mounted tub spout and controls with separate shower fittings

④ Contemporary tub spout and controls with a rain shower

⑤ Single-handle control for a tub spout with handheld shower

⑥ Dual controls for tub spout with handheld shower

⑦ Curved single-handle control, tub spout, and diverter valve with handheld shower

⑧ Dual-handle controls with handheld shower

⑨ Contemporary chrome controls, tub spout, and handheld shower

⑩ Horizontal controls and handheld shower

⑪ Dual-lever controls and contemporary tub spout with handheld shower

⑫ Cross-style chrome handles and tub spout with wand-style handheld shower

⑬ Single-handle chrome controls and tub spout with handheld shower

⑭ Single-handle controls for tub spout with handheld shower

⑮ Flared tub spout, diverter, and single-handle control with handheld shower

⑯ Flat single-handle control and tub spout with handheld shower

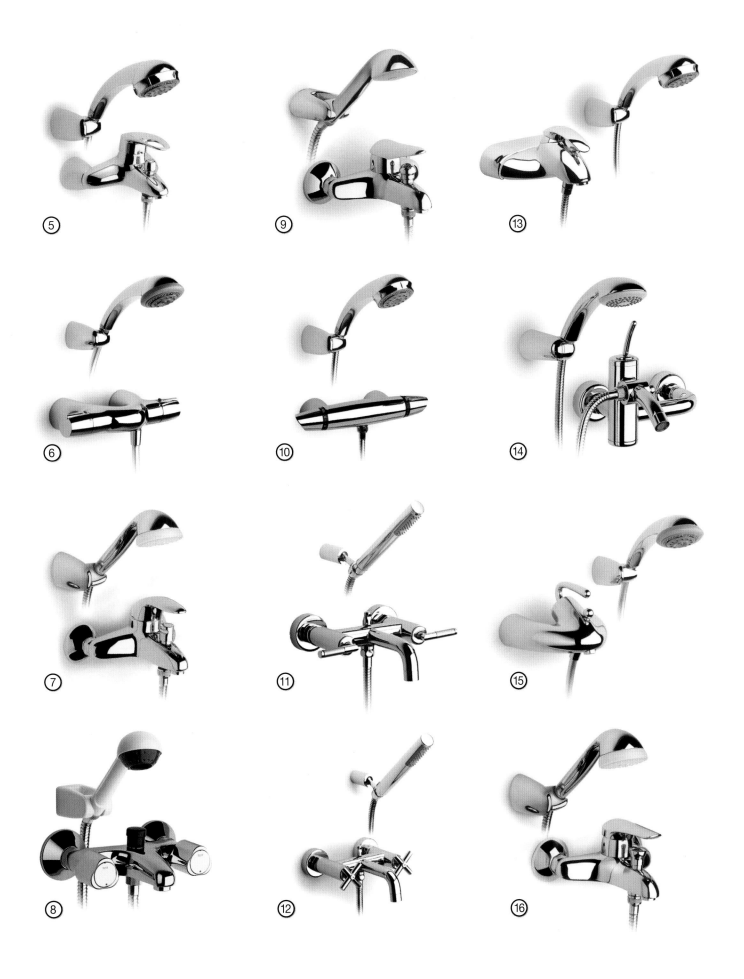

⑤

⑥

⑦

⑧

⑨

⑩

⑪

⑫

⑬

⑭

⑮

⑯

Steam Showers

Steam showers offer many of the benefits of a sauna as well as the pleasures of a luxury shower. They include steam generators that produce heated mist as well as controls that allow you to adjust the temperature and flow rate of the steam.

Steam shower enclosures are completely sealed to protect the room from excess heat and moisture. Their walls and doors go all the way to the ceiling or to the top of the unit. As a result, they don't have to be vented outside: their moisture doesn't enter the room, it simply drains away as the unit cools down.

(4)

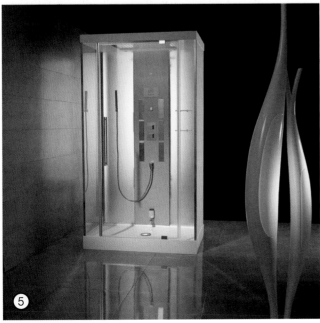

(5)

① A brass showerhead extends through the glass ceiling of this steam shower. The frameless glass enclosure is neatly tucked into the space at the end of the tub.

② Smoky glass panels and door enclose this compact steam shower, which includes a fan in its integral ceiling.

③ This curved, clear-glass enclosure fits into the corner of a bathroom, providing plenty of room to enjoy a steam shower within a relatively small space.

④ This rectangular enclosure includes a colored back panel to create visual interest and add color to the bathroom. The steam shower offers body jets and a rain shower.

⑤ Translucent back panels create a glowing environment for this steam shower, which also includes steam vents as well as a rainhead and body jets.

Wet Rooms

Wet rooms are open-plan bathrooms designed so that the entire space can be exposed to water. The floor is slightly raised to accommodate the waste plumbing and slightly sloped toward a centrally located drain. The shower is open to the rest of the room, which makes it barrier-free and easily accessible. Many designers suggest wall-hung fixtures and furnishings to keep the floor uncluttered, which adds to the spacious, open feeling of a wet room.

Wet rooms require excellent ventilation to help them dry out between uses. Because the floor will be wet, the floor coverings must be non-slip. Radiant heating in the floor helps control moisture and makes the room more pleasant to use.

The materials involved in wet rooms tend to be extremely heavy, so it is important the rooms have enough structural support to bear the extra weight.

① This gorgeous wet room has solid-surface walls and specially treated wood floors. The stainless-steel sink and chrome towel warmer stand up well to splashes and moisture from the adjacent shower.

② Dramatic slate tile covers the walls and floor of this stunning wet room. The vanity and shower areas are defined by a change in the size and shape of the tile.

③ This minimalist wet room is covered in two colors of ceramic tile and accessorized by sleek fixtures and fittings.

④ Glass block and glass mosaic tile adorn the sweeping curves of the walls in this wet room.

⑤ A curved glass panel contains the spray from the shower to one corner of this wet room.

Accessories

When it comes to shower accessories these days, the only limits are your imagination and budget. Truly, almost anything goes. From touch-controlled computer screens and televisions to speakerphones and entertainment systems, if it can be protected from moisture a designer somewhere has included it in a shower area.

The most practical and necessary shower accessories include benches and shelves. Although most people don't sit down to shower, benches are invaluable for those moments when you need a place to rest, especially while shaving or exfoliating. Shelves offer places to put toiletries and bathing necessities while you shower.

Audio systems are another popular shower accessory. Water-resistant speakers deliver music to the enclosure, giving you yet another reason to sing in the shower.

① A simple bench offers a resting spot for soap and shampoo as well as a place to rest on while shaving.

② High-quality audio speakers turn this enormous shower into a sound stage for one…or more!

③ A wood bathmat and chrome stool make this shower area more functional as well as more attractive.

④ Shower trays can be more than functional. They become decorative elements when they're as attractive as this stylish model.

⑤ This wooden bench can be folded down for use or returned to its upright position, a space-saving feature bathers truly appreciate.

Shower trays, sometimes called bases or pans, form the basis of many showers and establish their size and shape. They can vary from compact squares to spacious rectangular models and five-sided designs. They are made from a variety of materials, such as acrylic, glass, ceramic, wood, and stone. The type, size, and shape of the tray you choose depends entirely on the space and budget available for the shower itself.

① Square molded tray with center drain
② Oval recess centered in a rectangular tray with a center drain
③ Compact five-sided tray designed for a corner shower
④ Quadrant-shaped tray for a space-saving corner shower with a curved front
⑤ Ridged stone tray with stainless-steel grill leading to the drain
⑥ Simple rectangular tray with rectangular drain in the corner
⑦ Molded rectangular tray with octagonal drain hole in the corner
⑧ Molded tray designed for drying area of a walk-in shower
⑨ Quadrant tray with molded texture and corner drain access
⑩ Quadrant tray with beveled lip, polka-dot texture, and corner drain
⑪ Compact rectangular tray with central front drain
⑫ Rectangular tray with shaped floor and corner drain
⑬ Flared recess within a square tray
⑭ Quadrant tray with beveled edges, textured floor, and corner drain
⑮ Square tray with semi-circular recess
⑯ Quadrant recess within square tray
⑰ Bell-shaped recess within quadrant tray
⑱ Two-tone tray with horizontal slits leading to drain access

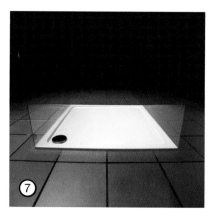

⑨

⑬

⑯

⑩

⑰

⑪

⑭

⑫

⑮

⑱

Saunas

Enthusiasts have proclaimed their health benefits for centuries, but until recently, all but the most dedicated had to travel to a health club or other commercial facility to enjoy a sauna. However, since the early 1990s, homeowners have been adding saunas to their bathrooms in increasing numbers. New technology, self-contained units, and the availability of affordable sauna kits are driving this trend.

The most widely reported of the many benefits attributed to saunas include: relieving tension and stress, reducing joint pain, soothing allergies and sinus congestion, removing toxins from the body, enhancing the complexion, and improving cardiovascular health. Some would argue that reports of these health benefits may be slightly exaggerated, but even the cynics can't deny how much simple pleasure saunas bring to life.

Traditional saunas are small rooms designed to withstand high temperatures and extremes in humidity control. They are built from aromatic wood, such as cedar or hemlock, and may include little other than a simple bench or two and a heat source. The heat source may be powered by wood, electricity, natural gas, or propane.

Infrared saunas use light to warm the body without warming the air surrounding it. These saunas are portable, easy to assemble, and remarkably energy efficient. They are also easy to clean and maintain.

Steam saunas—self-contained units with steam generators and sealed doors that contain the humidity—are multi-function, space-saving marvels of technology. Most require little more space than a luxurious shower and few special considerations other than connection to the bathroom's electrical circuits and plumbing lines.

Adding a home sauna can be as simple as assembling a two-piece kit and plugging it into a standard outlet. On the other hand, it can be as elaborate as commissioning a specially designed, custom-built unit that requires plumbers and electricians as well as skilled craftspeople to assemble and install. These saunas sometimes include music systems and aromatherapy units.

Saunas are safe and beneficial for most, but not all, users. People with diabetes, heart disease, high blood pressure, metal implants, or severe varicose veins are often cautioned about using saunas. The best advice is to consult your doctor before adding a sauna to your bathroom, especially if you fall into any of the categories mentioned.

Opposite: This stylish sauna has it all: heat, steam, and an integral shower.

Below: Simplicity is the hallmark of a traditional sauna. All that is truly required is a heater, bench, and bucket of water.

Types, Sizes, and Styles

Saunas can be divided into three main types: traditional (wet and dry), infrared, and steam saunas. Although debate rages about which is the best, it's mostly a matter of taste.

Traditional saunas can be divided into dry or wet saunas. Dry saunas use gas or electric heating units to warm the air to between 150 and 200°F (65 and 95°C). Their low humidity levels—typically near zero percent—make it possible for the body to tolerate these temperatures.

Wet saunas are operated between 110 and 115°F (43 and 46°C). Their heating units typically are topped by a pile of stones. Users ladle or sprinkle water onto the stones to produce steam.

Infrared saunas use a special spectrum of light to warm the body. They operate between 100 and 130°F (38 and 54°C). There is no added humidity.

Steam saunas are self-contained units that include steam generators rather than heating units.

① Four-person infrared sauna with comfortable seating and elegant details.

② Steam sauna with fixed and handheld showers as well as body jets. Includes shelves, a seat, and chromatherapy lighting.

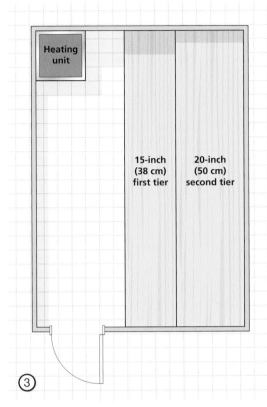

③

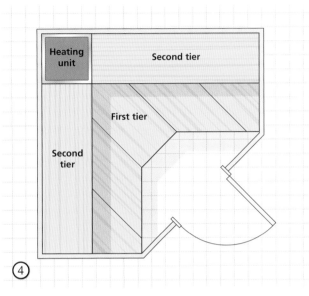

④

③ Convenient layout for a 5 x 8 foot (1.5 x 2.5 m) sauna. Two benches provide plenty of seating and room to lie down. The second level puts users higher in the sauna, where the temperatures are greater.

④ Layout for a compact, 4 x 4 foot (1.2 x 1.2 m) sauna to accommodate two people. Angled benches make the most of a small space.

⑤ Dry sauna lined with aromatic wood. Notice the wood guards surrounding the heating unit, preventing accidental contact with its surfaces.

⑤

Traditional Saunas

Traditional saunas may be dry or wet, but typically are lined with aromatic wood and include wood benches and floors.

People who prefer dry saunas find that the extreme heat promotes sweating and, therefore, quick detoxification. The sweat evaporates quickly, cooling the body enough to tolerate the heat.

Fans of wet saunas prefer the lower temperatures and the moisture provided by the steam, which hydrates the skin and soothes the respiratory system. The humidity levels are controlled by how much water one adds to the stones on top of the heating unit. The high humidity levels of wet saunas can promote the growth of mildew unless they are cleaned carefully and often.

The heating units for traditional saunas may be powered by wood or electricity as well as natural gas or propane. Wood and gas units must be vented outside the house. Few bathrooms have a gas line in place, but one can be added fairly easily in most cases. Small electric sauna units can be plugged into standard outlets, but larger ones must be wired into the electrical system.

②

①

③

(4)

① A self-contained, dry sauna can easily be assembled in place. This one includes two benches and a corner heating unit.

② This inviting sauna includes a light fixture in the corner. While not strictly necessary in saunas with glass doors and panels such as these, interior lighting is a pleasant addition.

③ Steam is produced by ladling water onto hot stones, such as the ones atop the heating unit in this wet sauna.

④ This built-in sauna, which takes advantage of the surrounding wood floor, was designed to fit precisely into the room's available space.

⑤ This large-capacity model has three benches on one side and two on the other. With its large expanse of glass and generous size, even a crowd wouldn't feel crowded.

(5)

(1)

Infrared Saunas

Infrared saunas are newer on the market, but they're gaining popularity rapidly. These saunas use light to warm the body. Advocates say that because they operate at lower temperatures, infrared saunas are safer for people with cardiovascular problems and less expensive to install and operate than traditional saunas.

Infrared saunas do not require special plumbing or wiring and do not have the maintenance issues related to the moist environment of wet saunas.

(2)

③

⑤

① Individual infrared sauna styled to resemble a cabinet or armoire.

② Traditional-looking unit designed for multiple users.

③ Two-person, cabinet-style sauna.

④ This reclining sauna is particularly appropriate for people who have difficulty being confined in small spaces.

⑤ Medium-sized sauna built into a custom-designed alcove.

④

Steam Saunas

The form may be new, but the function of steam saunas certainly is not. People have been enjoying steam baths since the days of the Roman Empire. Steam is known to hydrate the skin, clear the lungs, and help the body rid itself of toxins.

Many modern units combine the health benefits of steam with the convenience of a shower. They produce billows of steam on command and can be adjusted to the temperature and humidity level the user prefers. Many also include a wide range of amenities, such as handheld showers, multiple body jets, and even audio speakers.

Steam saunas can be quite heavy and may require reinforced floors or extra bracing in the wall framing. Check all specifications and make sure your steam sauna is adequately supported.

① Steam sauna with fixed and handheld showers, body jets, seat, shelves, and special lighting.

② Custom-built, tiled steam sauna with steam jets and custom-designed benches.

③ One-person steam sauna with overhead shower, built-in shelves, and seat.

④ Two-person steam sauna with two handheld showers, speakerphone, radio, aromatherapy, chromatherapy, and foot massager.

⑤ Two-person thermostatic steam sauna with fixed and handheld showers, body jets, multiple shelves, radio, and lights.

⑥ Two-person steam sauna with thermostatic controls, fixed and handheld showers, body jets, radio, lights, and mirror.

③

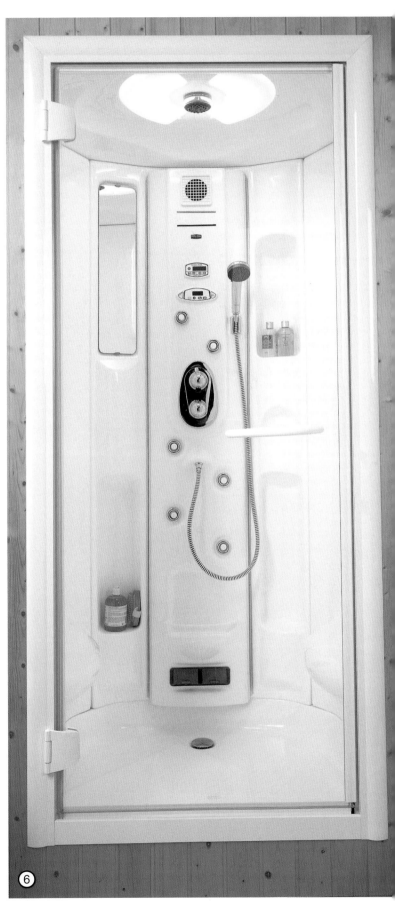

④

⑤

⑥

Fixtures

Fixtures—sinks and toilets—have undergone radical design changes in recent years. Traditionally, the emphasis has been on function, but we've seen a revolution in the market over the past few years. Today's designs act as ornaments and plumbing fixtures, in nearly equal parts. The materials used have changed nearly as much as the designs. Far beyond cultured marble and porcelain, today's choices include glass, stainless steel, natural stone, and even wood.

The design revolution has produced an enormous, and sometimes overwhelming, variety of fixtures. More than ever, it's necessary to balance practicality with beauty, innovation with usability. A hand-blown glass sink may be gorgeous, but can you shave in it? A square or rectangular toilet may suit your design aesthetic, but is it comfortable? Bathroom fixtures must fit the available space, the room scheme, and—more than anything—the people who use them.

Manufacturers now realize that one size does not fit all. Universal design, an effort to make homes work for all people at all stages of life, has played a central part in the revolution in fixture design. For example, sinks designed with side fittings (faucets and handles) are especially appropriate for children and people who use wheelchairs. Taller toilets are comfortable for people who have knee or hip issues. Features like these are incorporated into attractive fixtures that offer a sophisticated combination of accessibility and style.

A good fit involves more than size and shape. The materials of fixtures should be compatible with your lifestyle. Compare the characteristics of various materials and the maintenance they require before investing in fixtures. For example, it's important to know that an extreme swing in temperature can cause glass sinks to crack, or that honed stone has a mat finish very different from the shiny surface of polished stone. This type of information may not change your mind about a fixture, but it will help you make realistic buying decisions. Finally, consider the fixture's quality.

In addition to traditional retail outlets, bathroom fixtures are available from warehouse outlets, Internet websites, and auction sites. Carefully research suppliers and be wary of fixtures selling at rock-bottom prices. Make sure you're getting the quality you seek and know the warranties available before making purchases. In this chapter, we'll look closely at the various styles and types of sinks and toilets, as well as the characteristics of the materials available.

Opposite: These sleek sinks, with geometric shapes and their drain slits, are beautiful examples of contemporary design. Shallow basins like this are best suited for use by adults.

Below: This two-piece toilet is operated by a flush lever on the top of the tank, an innovation that enhances its clean, contemporary lines.

Types and Styles

Sinks are categorized according to how and where they are installed.

Pedestal and console sinks are attached to walls. Pedestals rarely provide functional support for sinks—they're mostly decorative.

Wall-hung sinks are mounted directly on walls. They're especially useful in small bathrooms.

Vanity-mounted sinks are attached to a countertop, which in turn is connected to a cabinet or a piece of freestanding furniture.

Toilets are available in several types, and may be mounted on walls or floors as well.

Two-piece toilets have separate tanks and bowls connected with bolts. They are easy to install and typically cheaper than comparable one-piece models.

One-piece toilets integrate the bowl and tank. They offer a streamlined appearance, and are easy to clean. They are often wall hung.

① This contemporary wall-hung sink and two-piece toilet make excellent use of space. Design standards suggest there should be 18 inches (45 cm) from the centerline of the toilet to the nearest fixture or wall.

② Wall-hung sinks are great for uncluttered floor space, but most offer little storage. That can be remedied with accessories, such as the towel ring and soap dispenser shown here.

③ This washbowl-style sink rests on a wood countertop. Deep basins reduce splashing, which makes it easier to maintain counters and floors.

④ The edges of this elongated sink rest on the counter. The joint between the sink and countertop must be kept watertight, usually with silicone caulk.

⑤ Vessel sinks are often coordinated with surface- or wall-mounted faucets and fittings. Sinks like this have to be thoughtfully installed to make them comfortable to use. Users must be able to reach the center of the basin as well as the faucet handles.

⑥ One-piece, wall-mounted toilets complement contemporary bathrooms. They use space efficiently and are typically very easy to clean.

Pedestal and Console Sinks

Although pedestal and console sinks appear to be freestanding, most are actually attached to a wall and must be supported by sturdy blocking. These sinks, which are available in styles ranging from traditional to ultra-modern, typically offer plenty of style and grace within modest amounts of floor space.

Pedestal sinks have pillar-type bases, most of which do little more than shield the plumbing from view. Console sinks consist of a basin surrounded by a base, typically one with two to four legs. In most cases, both pedestal and console sinks are two-piece units.

Pedestal and console sinks can be lovely, but their basic design limits the amount of storage or counter space they offer. If you choose one, be sure to double up on storage elsewhere in the bathroom.

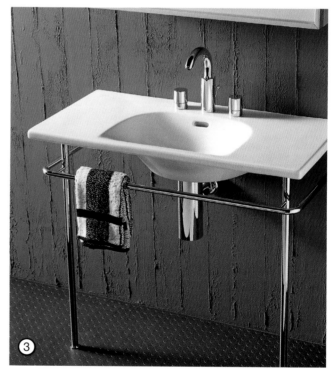

① The wood base of this freestanding console sink offers welcome storage for bathroom necessities.

② An integral backsplash protects the wall behind this pedestal sink, and gives it an interesting, traditional shape.

③ Generous decks on each side of this console sink provide plenty of room to place toiletries and cosmetics as you get ready for the day. The chrome base offers towel storage, too.

④ A subtle wood deck below the basin blends into the background, offering counter space without compromising the style of this unique pedestal sink.

⑤ This simple white pedestal sink glows against the deep-blue background of the wet wall, which houses the water supply and drain lines.

⑥ The eye-catching design of this one-piece sink speaks for itself. Although it appears to be freestanding, it is attached to the wall for support and safety.

⑦ A polished stainless-steel basin and pedestal shine in this contemporary setting. Polished surfaces, which show smudges and water spots, are better suited to guest baths or bathrooms used by meticulous adults.

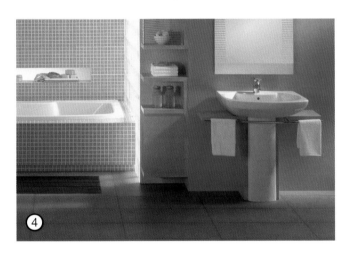

Pedestal sinks are available in heights from 32 to 36 inches (80 to 90 cm), which is determined by the height of the bases. Carefully evaluate various heights before deciding on a particular model. Lower sinks are more comfortable for children and petite adults; higher sinks work well for tall people. Although it's rarely possible to lower the height of a base, raising one is fairly straightforward. Simply install the sink on a platform.

Before shopping for a pedestal sink, evaluate the position of the existing plumbing, especially the distance from the wall to the front of the pipes. Choosing a unit with a base that fits your plumbing avoids the need to change the supply or drain lines.

Many pedestal sinks are manufactured with holes drilled to accommodate surface-mounted fittings. Make sure the unit you choose works with the fittings you have in mind. Traditional styles typically have three holes, while many contemporary styles are made with one hole in anticipation of a single-handle faucet.

① Contemporary rectangular basin
② Round-front basin
③ Streamlined oval basin with backsplash
④ Large rectangular basin with side decks
⑤ Oval basin with back deck
⑥ Extended-front, oval basin
⑦ Deep oval basin
⑧ Contemporary basin with towel-bar accessory
⑨ Space-efficient, rounded basin
⑩ Straight-lined, rectangular basin
⑪ Contemporary deep basin
⑫ Oval basin with column-style pedestal
⑬ Fountain-like pedestal and basin

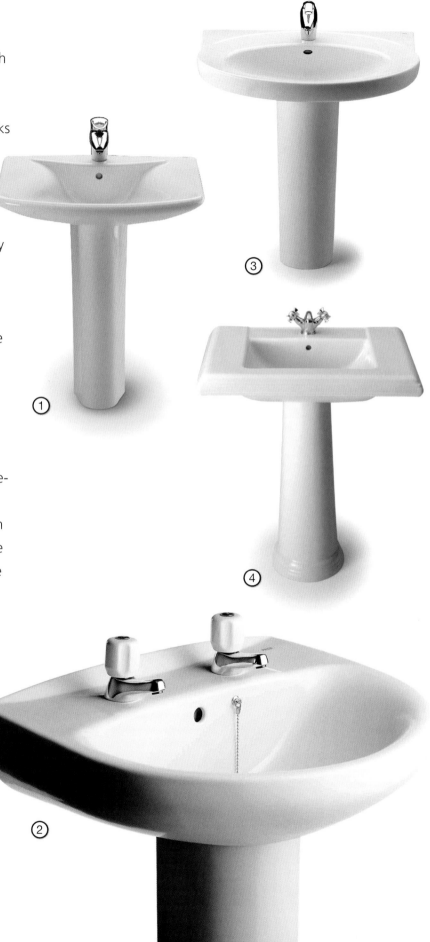

5

8

11

6

9

12

7

10

13

Wall-hung Sinks

Wall-hung sinks have become more popular than ever in recent years because they combine stylish looks with practicality. By virtue of being attached to walls rather than set into vanities, wall-hung sinks take less floor space—and less visual space—than other types of sinks. This helps make small bathrooms feel larger and large baths feel positively luxurious. It also provides easy access for wheelchairs.

Pipes and plumbing fittings are clearly visible beneath many wall-hung sinks. Some designs actually highlight the plumbing by incorporating stylish fittings or pipe covers. Others use decorative shields to conceal them. In bathrooms designed for wheelchair accessibility, it's a good idea to protect users from hot metal pipes with insulated covers or shields.

① Dual faucets on a single, oversized basin let two people use this sink at one time. The deep walls of this basin conceal the plumbing, leaving only clean lines.

② A glass counter extends from this integral glass sink, contributing work space. A wall-hung cabinet offers additional storage.

③ This porcelain sink includes a stylish plumbing shield that appears as part of the overall design rather than an add-on or embellishment.

④ This narrow sink could fit the smallest of rooms. The basin itself is considerably more shallow than the sink appears.

⑤ Wide decks offer counter space on either side of this contemporary beauty. A chrome rail protects users without completely concealing the lovely fittings.

⑥ The elongated oval of the drain highlights the shape of this sink. Shallow basins, such as this one, are prone to splashing and are best suited to bathrooms used mostly by adults.

⑤

④

⑥

Wall-hung sinks have another major advantage: they can be installed at any height that suits you. Sinks for children and seated users are mounted about 30 inches (75 cm) above the floor. Sinks for typical adults are mounted about 36 inches (90 cm) above the floor. In bathrooms with enough space for two sinks, universal design guidelines suggest mounting them at different heights to serve all users.

① Narrow basin with side decks
② Deep rectangular basin
③ Rectangular basin set lengthwise
④ Contemporary basin with plumbing shield and towel bar
⑤ Porcelain basin on wood base
⑥ Deep square basin with drying-rack accessory
⑦ Elegant contemporary basin
⑧ Irregular basin with extended side decks
⑨ Basin with built-in backsplash
⑩ Simple basin with plumbing shield
⑪ Rectangular basin with sloping sides
⑫ Rounded-front rectangular basin with plumbing shield
⑬ Small, round basin with extended decks
⑭ Square basin within oval deck
⑮ Corner sink with side deck
⑯ Rounded rectangular basin with extended side deck
⑰ Simple rectangular basin with rounded front
⑱ Oval basin with back deck
⑲ Deep square basin designed for side-mounted faucet
⑳ Flared basin with plumbing shield

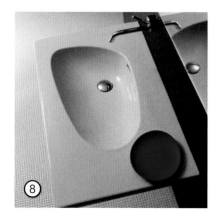

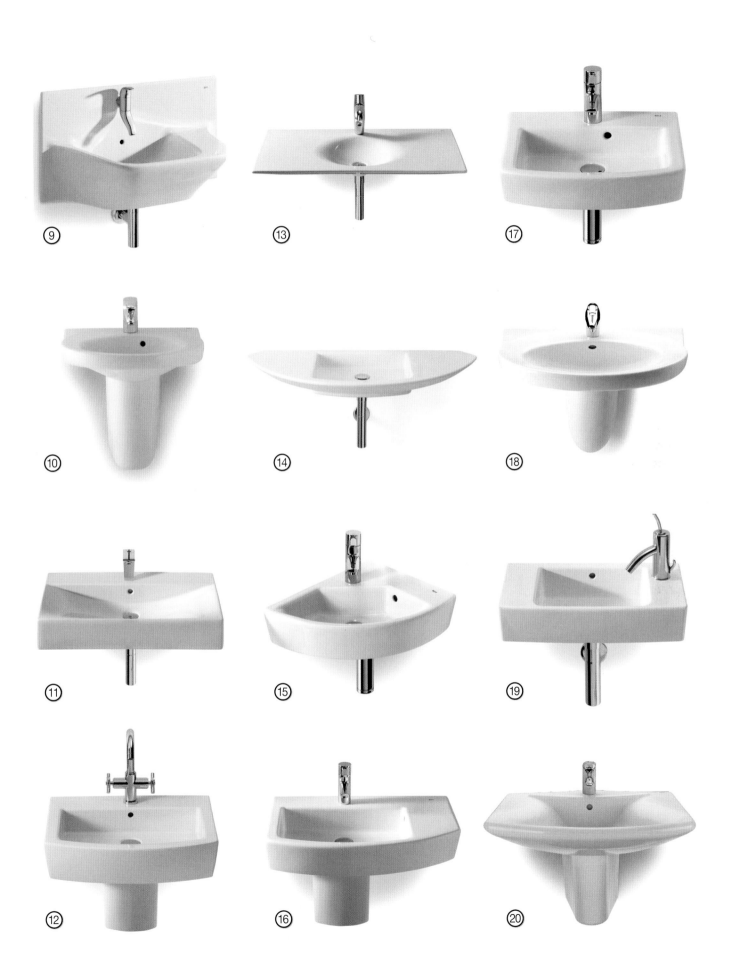

⑨
⑩
⑪
⑫
⑬
⑭
⑮
⑯
⑰
⑱
⑲
⑳

Vanity-mounted Sinks

Design trends come and go, but vanity-mounted sinks remain popular. Paired with cabinets or some other type of vanity, they combine counter space and storage, and are available in a range of styles.

Self-rimming sinks have rolled edges that rest directly on the counter. They are inexpensive and easy to install, but the joint between the sink and counter can be difficult to clean and maintain.

Flush-mounted sinks sit flush with the surface of the counter.

Undermount sinks are installed under the edges of the counter. The exposed edges must be finished and water resistant.

Integral sinks are molded into the countertop. They're attractive, virtually seamless, and can be expensive. Stainless steel and solid-surface, such as Corian, are common materials.

Vessel sinks sit directly on the counter, with bases covering the drain cut-outs.

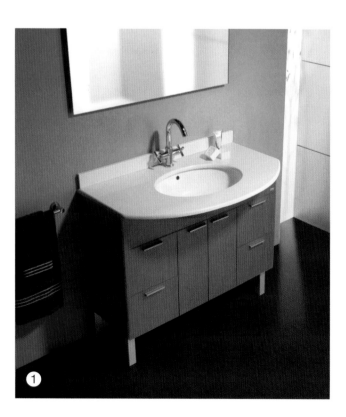

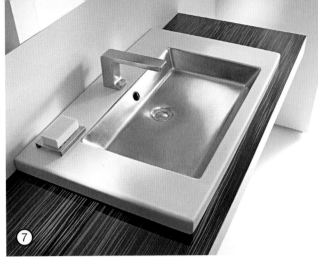

① This undermount sink fits neatly beneath a solid-surface countertop. The extended front edge of the counter adds a touch of drama to the otherwise plain arrangement.

② The graceful shape of this vessel sink creates a nice contrast with the rectangular lines of the faucet that serves it.

③ An integral sink covers the top of this vanity. With no seams or joints, integral sinks are extremely easy to maintain.

④ A gray solid-surface countertop offers a lovely contrast to the white undermount sink.

⑤ Unlike many vessel sinks, which are round or oval, this unit includes a deep, rectangular basin set within a square mold.

⑥ Basically, this sink is a shallow basin set over a large tray, which acts as a splashguard.

⑦ An integral stainless-steel sink, this unit is a high-style, low-maintenance marvel.

Vanity-mounted sinks are especially popular in family and children's baths because they make it easy to contain large collections of toiletries and cosmetics, maybe even bubble bath and a rubber duck or two.

It's possible to adapt chests and other pieces of furniture to hold vanity-mounted sinks. The chief requirement for this type of transformation is that the countertop be well supported. After that, anything goes.

① Square vanity-mounted sink with base
② Square self-rimming sink
③ Rectangular undermounted sink
④ Rounded self-rimming sink with extended front
⑤ Rectangular vanity-mounted sink on glass counter
⑥ Oval undermounted sink
⑦ Oval self-rimming sink
⑧ Shell-shaped novelty sink
⑨ Oval self-rimming sink with extended faucet base
⑩ Oval self-rimming sink with faucet base
⑪ Round self-rimming sink
⑫ Rectangular integral sink
⑬ Oval vanity-mounted sink with backsplash
⑭ Self-rimming sink with flared basin
⑮ Oval self-rimming sink with extended rear deck
⑯ Self-rimming sink with half-rounded basin
⑰ Flared basin in self-rimming sink
⑱ Self-rimming sink with extended side deck
⑲ Vanity-mounted sink with square basin
⑳ Deep basin on undermounted sink

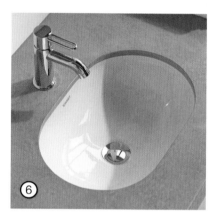

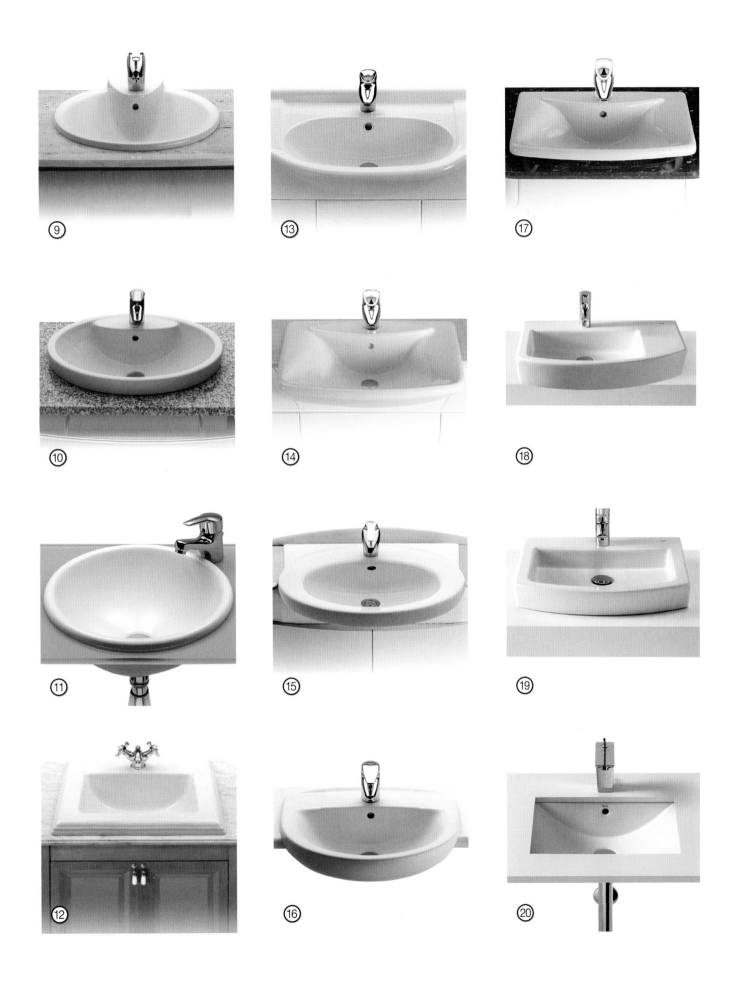

Vessel Sinks

Vessel sinks, washbowl-like basins that sit directly on counters, are one of this century's hottest trends in bathrooms. Some blur the lines between fixture and art, and adding one positively transforms a bathroom. Many are created by hand from glass or stone. Others are manufactured from glass, stone, metal, or porcelain.

Most vessel sinks are approximately 15 to 20 inches (38 to 50 cm) in diameter and between 5 and 6 inches (12 and 15 cm) high. Although they're excellent choices for powder rooms, guest baths, or bathrooms used by adults, it's important to realize that vessel sinks may not work in family bathrooms. They are prone to splashing and the materials used tend to require more maintenance than those used for less artistic sinks. Deeper sinks usually produce less splashing.

① A slightly irregular shape gives this porcelain bowl a hand-thrown appearance. The higher front helps keep water from spilling onto the floor.

② Because they're so striking, vessel sinks tend to set a bathroom's theme. The color scheme here was taken from the dark smoky gray color of the vessel sink.

③ This deep porcelain vessel has an overflow drain, a feature that's not very common on vessel sinks.

④ The pebbly surface of this sink camouflages water spots, but most manufacturers recommend wiping out glass vessels after each use.

⑤ This honed stone vessel complements the room's tile and other surfaces. The mat surface of honed stone gives vessels the appearance of sculpture.

⑥ A polished metal vessel provides a counterpoint to the rough-hewn wood of this bathroom.

④

⑤

③

⑥

Vessel sinks are made from a wide variety of materials, each with its own characteristics and properties.

Vitreous china bowls are impervious to stains and can stand up to virtually any type of cleanser. They are extremely durable, but can chip and crack over time.

Glass vessels are surprisingly sturdy. A process known as tempering makes the glass five to seven times stronger than regular glass. Even so, most designers agree that glass vessels are best suited for bathrooms used by adults or children older than 10 years old.

Ceramic basins are often produced by potters and hand-painted or glazed by artists. Although they are reasonably durable, they are more prone to damage than vitreous china and require more gentle treatment.

Metal bowls are durable, easy to clean, and hide dirt well. Brushed surfaces are easier to maintain than shiny ones. Stainless steel stands up to everyday use, but pewter, nickel, and brass are softer and require considerable maintenance.

Solid-surface materials are extremely durable and resistant to stains and scratches. Surface damage can be sanded out fairly easily.

① Round porcelain bowl
② Oval porcelain vessel
③ Square porcelain vessel with rounded base
④ Rectangular vessel resting on four legs
⑤ Tempered glass bowl
⑥ Porcelain apothecary bowl
⑦ Polished brass bowl
⑧ Brushed stainless-steel bowl
⑨ Deep rectangular basin with sloped sides
⑩ Honed stone bowl
⑪ Porcelain basin with chrome base
⑫ Stone bowl with textured rim

Double Sinks

Double sinks are important conveniences for busy couples. No waiting in line to brush your teeth in the morning, no shaving cream drying on your face as you wait your turn at the sink. With double sinks, there's room for everyone.

Double sinks are most functional when there's at least 30 inches (75 cm) between the two basins, measured from centerline to centerline. Less distance is acceptable but will make it more difficult for two people to use the area at the same time.

Although it's the most common arrangement by far, it's not necessary for double sinks to be exactly the same. As long as they're made from the same materials and their sizes and shapes relate well to one another, there's no reason not to use, say, one vessel sink and one undermount or integral sink.

① Two integral sinks are molded into this compact countertop unit. The vanity includes two deep drawers, one for each sink.

② These deep basins, served by floor-mounted faucets, are separated by a broad expanse of counter space and storage.

③ Simple square basins mirror one another on this wall-hung counter. Ample storage elsewhere in the room keeps this area neat.

④ Adding a towel bar to one of these identical wall-hung sinks customizes it for the user.

⑤ This bathroom is truly made for two. There is plenty of room between and around the sinks and each is served by its own mirror, ledge space, towel ring, and light fixture.

⑥ The basins of this double pedestal sink are divided by an integral wall and little else. A sink like this might work better for children or a couple with flexible schedules than for two adults trying to use them at the same time.

Two-piece Toilets

Two-piece toilets consist of a base and tank that are bolted together during installation. Over time, these bolts can corrode and leaks can develop between the tank and base. However, the design of two-piece toilets has withstood the test of time most admirably.

Two-piece units are often less expensive than comparable one-piece toilets. Round bowls use less space than the elongated versions, but the elongated bowls are considered to be more comfortable for adults. Most two-piece toilets are sold without seats and lids, which must be purchased separately.

As water conservation efforts have forced toilet manufacturers to reduce the amount of water used per flush, new designs have emerged. Taller, slimmer tanks improve flushing power, as do the units that increase the pressure of the water flowing through the system.

① This model features a push-button flush lever on top of a tall, slim tank. Manufacturers often offer bidets designed to coordinate with toilet styles.

② Toilet designers are making use of unusual materials and shapes. This porcelain base is attached to a brushed, stainless-steel tank. The height of the tank is more than a design feature: it actually improves the toilet's flushing power.

③ This unit is a modified version of a Victorian water closet. Its elevated tank is connected to the base by a polished brass pipe.

④ A traditional two-piece toilet demonstrates why this style has endured for decades. It is simple, functional, and attractive.

⑤ The slim tank of this contemporary design contrasts nicely with the chunkiness of the base. Its lines and shape complement the pedestal sink.

③

⑤

④

The first consideration when choosing a toilet should be the quality of the flush.

Gravity-flush toilets use gravity to move water from the tank.

Washdown toilets have large traps, which make them less likely to clog.

Vacuum-assisted toilets have two smaller tanks within the main tank. A vacuum is created between the tanks and enhances the flush

Pressure-assisted toilets use compressed air to push the water and waste through the system.

Dual-flush toilets have two flush levers, one for solid waste and one for liquid waste. They conserve water by using less water to flush liquids.

① Slimline tank and rounded bowl
② Streamlined contemporary tank and bowl
③ Traditional-style toilet with elongated bowl
④ Slant bowl with rounded front
⑤ Low-rise tank with rounded bowl
⑥ Clean-lined base and low-rise tank
⑦ Wall-hung toilet with tank-mounted flush lever
⑧ Slimline tank with tank-mounted flush lever and elongated base
⑨ Elongated base with tank-mounted flush lever
⑩ Elongated base with rounded seat
⑪ Square-front base and slimline tank
⑫ Elongated base with rounded front
⑬ Contemporary toilet with angled, elongated front
⑭ High-rise tank with rounded base
⑮ Elongated base with rounded front and tank-mounted flush lever
⑯ Square toilet with high-rise tank

⑨

⑩

⑪

⑫

⑬

⑭

⑮

⑯

One-piece and Wall-hung Toilets

One-piece and wall-hung toilets are common in contemporary and minimalist settings. Their self-contained nature makes them easy to clean and maintain. Unlike two-piece toilets, most one-piece and wall-hung fixtures are sold with seats and lids. These are designed to fit the unit's shape, which is often less universal than that of comparable two-piece fixtures.

Like wall-hung models, one-piece toilets sit close to the wall, which makes good use of floor space. More often than not, they offer the comfort of elongated bowls.

Wall-hung toilets are attached to the wall rather than supported by the floor. To ensure their stability, a steel support frame must be hidden within the furniture unit or framed into the wall. This allows you to adjust the toilet to a comfortable height.

②

①

③

① The flush levers for this dual-flush, wall-hung toilet are located on the wall above. The short flush, designed for liquid waste, uses less water than the long flush.

② The rectangular shape of this toilet echoes the shapes of the room's other fixtures. Unusual shapes like this may not be comfortable for all. Try one before buying it.

③ This toilet is attached to the cabinet rather than the wall. To do this, cabinets must be modified to support the toilet.

④ When closed, the lid of this unique piece conceals the toilet altogether.

⑤ A partial wall supports this simple unit. The framing support and plumbing necessary for such a unit should be designed and executed by experts.

⑥ This wall-hung unit fits into a relatively compact space and leaves room for the sink to be used, too.

Wall-hung toilets require special support. When shopping, ask for diagrams of the necessary support structure so you can evaluate possible placement in your bathroom.

With all styles of toilets, the power of the flush is a major factor when making a purchase. The only way to make an informed buying decision is to see a demonstration of the toilet's flushing power first. Retailers use simple objects, such as sponges or balls, to demonstrate a toilet's flush power.

① Wall-hung toilet with elongated bowl

② Wall-hung toilet with round bowl

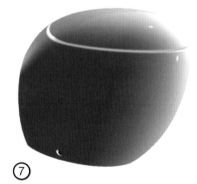

① Wall-hung toilet with elongated bowl
② Wall-hung toilet with round bowl
③ Rectangular base with elongated bowl
④ Rectangular base with comfort height seat
⑤ Wall-hung toilet with elongated base and rectangular front
⑥ Wall-hung toilet with elongated base and rounded front
⑦ Contemporary elliptical toilet
⑧ Wall-hung toilet with square base
⑨ Elongated base with extended lid
⑩ Elongated base with easy-clean design
⑪ Elongated bowl with pedestal-style base
⑫ Wall-hung toilet with elongated bowl
⑬ Wall-hung toilet base with traditional styling
⑭ Streamlined wall-hung toilet with easy access to water supply
⑮ Wall-hung toilet with pedestal-style base
⑯ Wall-hung toilet with deep base
⑰ Streamlined elongated base with rounded front
⑱ Contemporary wall-hung toilet with oval seat
⑲ Rounded-front, elongated wall-hung toilet
⑳ Streamlined elongated toilet with rounded front

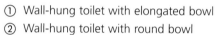

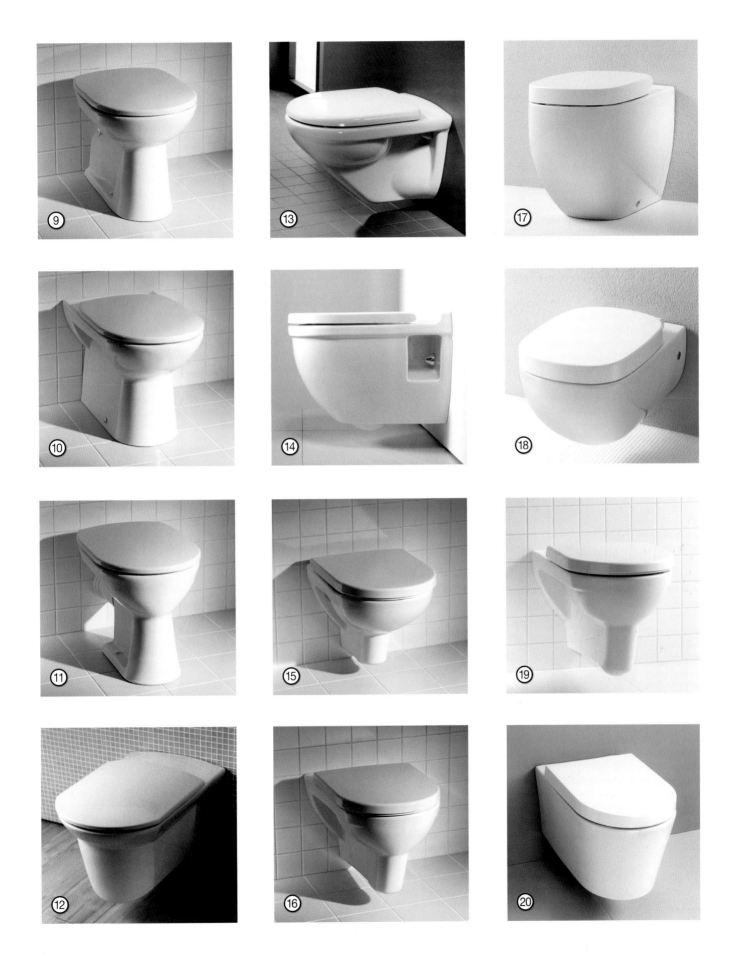

Storage and Furniture

The trend toward luxurious bathroom retreats has created dramatic changes in the storage and furnishings being used today. Standard cabinets and unimaginative storage pieces have given way to high-quality components designed to resemble custom furnishings. Actual furniture has moved into bathrooms, too. Shelf units, armoires, and even lounge chairs have become common. Today's bathroom furnishings are designed to hide their hard-working nature behind elegant exteriors. Look beyond their surfaces and you'll find an emphasis on storage, convenience, and, above all, comfort.

Whether your bathroom is designed to be a model of efficiency or a peaceful oasis, clutter is the enemy. Few things are more frustrating than digging through things you don't want in search of the ones you do.

Good organization starts with having places for your belongings. You simply cannot corral the towels, take control of the cosmetics, or keep a handle on the cleaning supplies without designating spaces to store them. Only through thoughtful combinations of furnishings can one hope to accommodate the accumulation of products and devices competing for space in most bathrooms.

Successful bathroom storage lets you display attractive pieces and keep less appealing—but necessary—items out of sight and still within easy reach. This requires a combination of open shelves, closed cabinets, and drawers.

The best way to select components that meet your daily needs is to make an inventory of the items in the bathroom and categorize them according to the appropriate type of storage. With an inventory in hand, it's much easier to evaluate the quantities and qualities of cabinets, drawers, and shelves necessary to create an efficient, comfortable atmosphere in your bathroom.

For decades, homebuilders have almost automatically repeated the same cabinet styles and colors from a home's kitchen in its bathrooms. No more! Today's relaxed, individualistic approach lets you blend colors, textures, and even eras in one room.

As the square footage assigned to bathrooms increases and amenities are added, homeowners are looking for more ways to enjoy these luxurious new spaces. The big news is that seating—chairs, loungers, ottomans, and even sofas—are being incorporated into today's bathrooms.

Despite the variety of pieces being used today, all bathroom furniture has one thing in common: it must be able to withstand the wet, humid conditions of bathrooms. High-quality materials and finishes are essential, as well as good care and maintenance.

Opposite: A wall-hung vanity reminiscent of a two-drawer file keeps essentials within reach of the sink in this high-tech atmosphere.

Below: Small cabinets equipped with casters can be rolled into place for use and then tucked out of sight until needed again.

Types and Styles

Bathroom storage components and furniture can be divided into three basic types and styles: built-in furniture and vanity units, wall units, and freestanding furniture. No one type or style is right for everyone or even every purpose in one bathroom—but each can contribute to the symphony.

Built-in furniture and vanity units are the melodies in most bathrooms. They typically include drawers and shelves, and can be fitted with specialized accessories like jewelry compartments, hampers, and tilt-out trays.

Wall units add harmony: storage areas for items that are necessary but not used every day.

Freestanding furniture pieces contribute grace notes and may be chosen as much for their looks as for their ability to be rearranged.

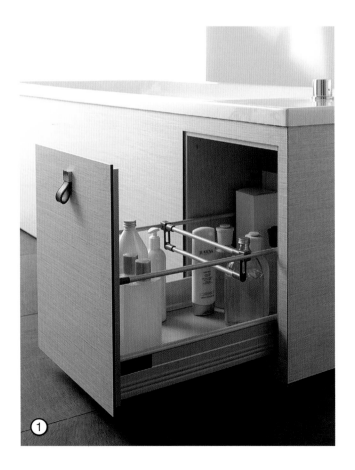

① Side rails and an interior divider keep the contents of the deep drawers of this vanity organized.

② A sleek vanity floats against the wall of this eclectic bathroom. Discreet handholds, which substitute for knobs or pulls, let users operate drawers with ease.

③ This freestanding vanity has been fitted with a counter and integral sink, a surprisingly simple operation.

④ Extended toe kicks position these cabinets at a comfortable height. The recessed mirror offers a nice balance for the larger center unit of the base.

⑤ This wall unit, positioned beside the shower, offers convenient storage for towels and toiletries.

⑥ A brightly colored vanity makes a bold statement that is as fundamental to this bathroom as the storage space it offers.

Built-in Furniture and Vanities

Built-in furniture and vanities are customized, in various ways, to fit specific spaces.

Ready-to-assemble units are sold in set sizes that can be configured to fit the room. These are usually the most affordable cabinets, but the range is limited.

Stock cabinets come in a range of sizes, typically in 3-inch (7.5-cm) increments to fit most bathrooms. Most offer a choice of doors, but drawers and shelving options can be limited.

Semi-custom pieces are made in hundreds of sizes, finishes, and styles so you can create your own combination of units and accessories. They range from simple and affordable to luxurious and expensive.

Custom furniture is built by craftspeople to fit the specifications of your room; for this reason it's the most expensive style.

① Tall cabinets that act as linen closets for the bathroom flank this finely crafted vanity.

② A combination of upper and lower cabinets as well as open shelves gives this bathroom superior storage capacity.

③ A raised area surrounding the sink provides room for additional drawers as well as an attractive backsplash.

④ Here, a wall of shallow cabinets plays host to the sink as well as the wall-hung toilet.

⑤ Custom-built shelves below the tub deck offer convenient storage for towels, toiletries, and bathing supplies.

⑥ Laminate can be formed into almost any shape, such as the curved sink front in this spectacular bath.

Built-in furniture and vanities are made in two basic styles:

Framed cabinets are common in period or traditional-style homes. The edges of their cases are covered with trim boards known as face frames. Doors may be set into these frames or laid over them.

Frameless cabinets are common in modern and contemporary-style homes. Because the cabinet box is not framed, the edges are banded for a finished appearance. Often with this style the drawers and doors are flush across the entire box, so that even if there were frames they would not be visible.

① Traditional-style framed vanity
② Contemporary frameless cabinets
③ Framed vanity and wall cabinets with period details
④ Vanity with pull-out drawers
⑤ Matching frameless, built-in vanities
⑥ Frameless vanity with translucent doors on each side
⑦ Frameless double vanity
⑧ Frameless, oval built-in vanity
⑨ Built-in vanity with extended shelf
⑩ Ultra-modern vanity and sliding doors
⑪ Double vanity with towel-bar accessory
⑫ Vanity with translucent sliding doors
⑬ Contemporary vanity with sliding doors
⑭ Built-in vanity with towel-bar accessory
⑮ Built-in vanity with translucent sliding doors and interior lights
⑯ Asymmetrical built-in vanity
⑰ Built-in, frameless vanity with wide, shallow drawers
⑱ Built-in corner vanity flanked by open shelves
⑲ Built-in vanity with accessorized door
⑳ Framed, shallow shelf unit built into custom vanity

Wall Units

Wall units add enormous storage potential without taking up a great deal of square footage. They range from small, medicine-chest type cabinets to large, armoire-like pieces. The open space below them means these furnishings—even large units—don't take up as much visual space as comparable built-in or freestanding cabinets. They work especially well in small bathrooms.

Wall units are supported by the wall framing. Walls supporting unusually large or heavy models may require additional blocking or reinforcement. Consult a contractor or manufacturer's product specifications for important building and safety requirements.

Many wall units are centered at eye-level, offering excellent display space. Units with glass doors, open shelves, or lights make particularly attractive displays.

① A combination of glass, mirrors, and metal in the center unit reflects and refracts light into the room.

② Reminiscent of school lockers, this spacious unit adds color as well as storage.

③ Two wall units surround a unique vanity with storage space.

④ Translucent glass lets the color of these linens shine through without allowing a clear view of the contents. It also obscures stray fingerprints or smudges.

⑤ Glass shelves take up little visual space, which leaves the focus on the attractive linens and toiletries in this cabinet.

⑥ This clever piece provides shelf space on top and the convenience of drop-down storage below, including a tissue dispenser.

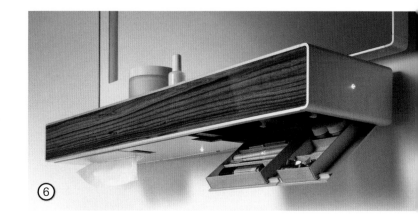

Wall units take advantage of the prime territory that ergonomic experts tell us is the most useful for storage—between hip and shoulder height.

At least one locked compartment is essential for medicine cabinets if children live in or visit your home. Although these cabinets aren't typically within easy reach of children, their lack of accessibility may intrigue children more than it protects them. If installing a lock isn't practical, add safety latches or other security devices. It really is better to be safe than sorry.

① Contemporary mirrored wall unit
② Mirrored backlit medicine cabinet
③ Mirrored unit with a series of small drawers
④ Mirror unit topped with wood-grain
⑤ Central mirror surrounded by open shelves
⑥ Mirror with slide-out drawer
⑦ Central shelf unit flanked by wood cabinets
⑧ Double wall units with wood grain and laminate
⑨ Tall unit with translucent glass doors
⑩ Two-toned wall unit
⑪ Burgundy doors within a wood-grain frame
⑫ Tall wood unit with adjustable glass shelves
⑬ Small wood unit with two translucent glass doors
⑭ Open shelves sandwiched between closed cabinets
⑮ Tall unit with stripes created by alternating wood stains
⑯ Two-drawer unit topped with a tray
⑰ One open glass-topped shelf, and one floating drawer

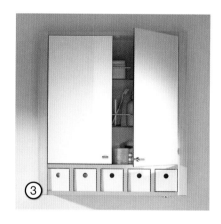

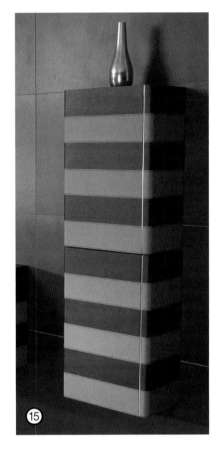

Freestanding Furniture

Adding freestanding furniture to bathrooms is one of the hottest trends of recent years, and no one expects the trend to change in the near future. Freestanding pieces can be used to fill large bathrooms with colors, shape, and texture or to experiment with new ideas or styles without the commitment of built-in pieces. In small bathrooms, they can combine function with high style.

The other wonderful part about freestanding furniture is that it can go with you if you move, so you can afford to invest in special pieces.

Incorporating freestanding furniture lets you combine the influences of different corners of the globe and different periods of time to create a glorious, eclectic mix. Unlike built-in furnishings, it's easy to rotate freestanding pieces into and out of a bathroom as the seasons change or the mood strikes you.

① A chrome-and-glass étagère provides display space beside the glass shower.

② A coffee-table-like platform holds towels and all manner of toiletries.

③ Tall, matching chests with deep drawers offer exceptional storage for towels, linens, and clothing.

④ A curio cabinet and quilt rack combine display and storage space with pure elegance.

⑤ The wood and glass display stand was built to complement the modified table used here as a vanity.

⑥ Modifications, such as removing drawers or adding countertops, are sometimes required when adapting freestanding pieces.

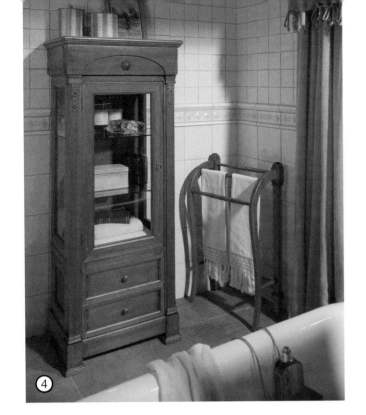

④

⑥

⑤

Freestanding furniture for bathrooms should be made with materials that stand up well to humidity. Many manufacturers now offer furniture that is especially designed for moist, warm conditions.

Metals, such as wrought iron, chrome, stainless steel, and nickel are excellent choices. Polycarbonates, resins, and glass work well, too. Wood is appropriate as long as the finish is adequate.

Extremes in temperature and moisture levels cause improperly finished wood to expand and contract, which can damage the finish or even the wood itself. But never refinish a fine antique without consulting an expert first—alterations can destroy its value.

① Metal display stand
② Chrome and glass display stand
③ Hand-lacquered wood cabinet
④ Wood and metal rolling cabinet
⑤ Wood and glass cabinet on casters
⑥ Rolling cosmetics case
⑦ Wood bench used as shelf
⑧ Wood stand used as vanity
⑨ Wood bench used as shelf
⑩ Parsons table used as vanity
⑪ Small laminate cabinet
⑫ Wood bookcase with translucent glass doors
⑬ Wood and laminate armoire
⑭ Wood and glass display unit
⑮ Chrome coat racks used for towel storage

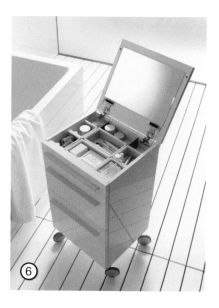

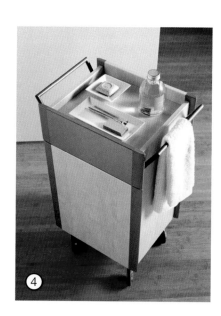

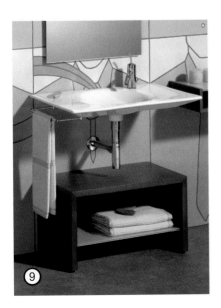

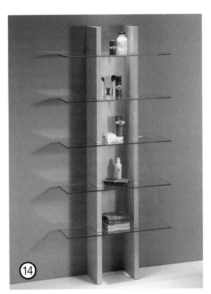

Faucets and Accessories

Faucets have always been a vital part of a bathroom, and while accessories are, by definition, small and non-essential, they nevertheless help the bathroom to function at its best. Today's faucets don't merely deliver water to sinks and tubs, and holders and dispensers, hooks, rings and bars, and mirrors don't just make the bathroom easier to use—they both add a design element. Today's faucets and accessories get the job done, but they do it with whole new levels of style and grace.

Well-chosen faucets and fittings can contribute as much to a bathroom's design as its fixtures. Given the right emphasis, wall-mounted faucets become art, and deck-mounted fittings become jewelry. The trick becomes matching the style, material, and finish to the design sensibility of the room.

When it comes to faucets and fittings, there are also logistics to consider. For example, vessel sinks require counter- or wall-mounted faucets, and some tubs come pre-drilled for deck-mounted fittings. You'll need to know whether sinks and tubs have pre-drilled holes, and, if so, how many and how far apart they are.

Once you have the logistics well in hand, it's time to consider materials and finishes. Be sure to coordinate them with the room's accessories. And, if you've already chosen light fixtures, take their finish into consideration as well. Not all fixtures and accessories have to match precisely, but they should complement one another. It would be unusual, for example, for brushed-nickel faucets and fittings to work well with polished-brass light fixtures. However, white ceramic faucets might be the perfect touch with polished-chrome towel bars and rings.

Before making final selections, examine the construction of the faucets and fittings you're considering. The most durable faucets have corrosion-resistant finishes, which makes them more durable and easier to maintain.

Like almost every other aspect of our lives, technology has changed bathrooms. You can buy mirrors that swivel, magnify, and resist fogging. And you can now fit televisions and touch-screen monitors that allow you to check stock quotes and even e-mail as you prepare for the day—or catch up with your favorite TV program as you relax in the bath.

Throughout this chapter you'll find information designed to help you select appropriate faucets and fittings as well as accessories that will make your bathroom as pleasant to look at as it is to use.

Opposite: A high-capacity, floor-mounted tub spout and hand shower stand ready beside this marvelous contemporary tub.

Below: A chrome train rack stores towels in plain sight and within easy reach.

Types and Styles

Faucets and fittings are divided into two categories: those designed for use with sinks and those created to serve bathtubs. Either may be wall-mounted or deck-mounted and may involve one or two handles in addition to the spout.

When choosing faucets and fittings, look for solid-brass construction, corrosion-resistant finishes, and ceramic disc valves, to ensure they last a long time.

Accessories include holders and dispensers, towel hooks, bars, rings, and mirrors. Towel hooks, bars, and rings present three choices for hanging your towels. Towel bars typically come in 18- and 24-inch (45- and 60-cm) lengths. Most rings are sized to hold hand towels rather than bath towels.

Bathroom mirrors may be framed or frameless. Framed mirrors do not have to be designed specifically for the bathroom as long as they have moisture-resistant finishes. Frameless mirrors are attached to the wall with special J-clips that must be secured to framing studs.

In addition to mirrors, all wall-mounted accessories must be attached to framing studs or secured with sturdy mounting hardware.

① Traditional-style, wall-mounted faucets and fittings serve this elegant freestanding tub.

② Brushed-nickel soap and tissue dispensers blend into this monochromatic setting.

③ Tub fittings in a combination of polished chrome and white ceramic match the tone of this traditional bath.

④ A polished-chrome hook holds a warm robe right beside the bathroom's entrance.

⑤ A wall-mounted tumbler is a handy place to keep your toothbrushes.

⑥ A simple, high-capacity tub spout and hand shower are well suited to this contemporary tub.

⑦ A waterproof shield protects this television from the moist environment of the bathroom.

Faucets and Fittings

Faucets and fittings must first be compatible with the fixtures they serve. Important considerations include the height and depth of the sink or tub as well as its capacity. Here are some specifics to keep in mind:

- High-capacity spouts fill large tubs more quickly.
- Waterfall spouts deliver appealing, flat streams of water.
- Gooseneck spouts are best suited to deep basins that will contain the inevitable splashes created from their greater height.
- Deck-mounted spouts must be long enough to reach the basin or tub.
- Wall-mounted spouts should reach to the center of a sink basin, above the drain.
- Lever handles are the easiest to use. They're great for children and especially useful for people with limited hand strength.
- Spouts for vessel sinks have to be tall enough to reach up and over the sink and still leave room for the sink to be used.

⑤

⑥

① A gooseneck spout delivers a flat stream of water to the center of this deep basin.

② Deck-mounted faucets with integral handles add little fuss to this minimalist setting.

③ Handheld showers are convenient for users of all sizes and abilities.

④ The traditional style of chrome and white ceramic is combined with a modern twist: a delightful waterfall spout.

⑤ Deep-brown ceramic risers provide lovely contrast with the golden glow of these fittings.

⑥ A wide waterfall spout fills this deep basin quickly.

⑦ This high-tech, high-capacity tap can be operated by remote control.

⑦

Match the faucets and fittings to the type of tub you've chosen.

Wall-mounted fittings are used with alcove and other tubs that are mounted against walls.

Deck-mounted fittings are mounted on flat surfaces—the side of the tub or a surrounding deck. The spout must be long enough to reach well into the tub.

Floor-mounted faucets are designed for freestanding tubs. Their risers, which are often exposed, must be sized to work with the height of the tub.

① Two-handle nickel faucet with handheld shower attachment
② Floor-mounted gooseneck faucet
③ Contemporary floor-mounted faucet and handheld shower
④ Floor-mounted faucet and shower attachment
⑤ Sleek, two-handled tub faucet and handheld shower
⑥ Deck-mounted faucet and handheld shower
⑦ Deck-mounted satin steel faucet with lever handles
⑧ Deck-mounted faucet with round handles
⑨ Single-handle tub spout
⑩ Wall-mounted spout with dial handles
⑪ Waterfall spout
⑫ Brass faucet with lever handles
⑬ Angular spout with lever handles
⑭ Deck-mounted gooseneck spout with lever handles
⑮ High-flow spout with lever handles
⑯ Single-handle spout
⑰ Waterfall spout and handheld shower
⑱ Deck-mounted, bridged faucet

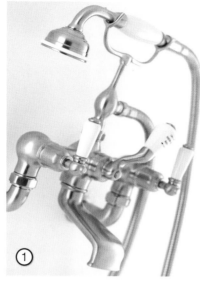

⑦

⑪

⑮

⑧

⑫

⑯

⑨

⑬

⑰

⑩

⑭

⑱

Sink faucets may be mounted on the wall, counter, or the sink itself. Deck-mounted fittings must match the configuration of the holes in the sink.

Centerset faucets require sinks with three holes set no more than 4 inches (10 cm) apart.

Single faucets are used with sinks that have one hole. Most have a single handle, but some have two handles attached to the sides of the spout.

Widespread faucets are controlled by two handles, each independent from the spout. They are used with three-hole sinks as well as mounted on counters behind sinks with no pre-drilled holes. Most have a reach (from one side to the other) of between 8 and 16 inches (20 and 40 cm).

① Individual hot and cold faucets
② Single-lever tall faucet
③ Motion-sensor faucet
④ Single-handle ceramic and steel faucet
⑤ Brushed steel, deck-mounted waterfall faucet
⑥ Single-hole faucet with integral handles
⑦ Single-hand chrome faucet
⑧ Widespread faucet with cross handles
⑨ Sweeping single-handle faucet
⑩ Tall faucet with single handle
⑪ Centerset faucet with dual handles
⑫ Centerset waterfall faucet
⑬ Gold-plated faucet with cross handles
⑭ Centerset faucet with side-mounted knobs
⑮ Single-handle faucet with top-mounted knob
⑯ Single-hole faucet with cross handles
⑰ Widespread faucet with bar handles
⑱ Wall-mounted faucet with control knobs
⑲ Pewter bridged faucet with cross handles
⑳ Bridged faucet with lever handles

①

⑤

②

⑥

③

⑦

④

⑧

⑨

⑬

⑰

⑩

⑭

⑱

⑪

⑮

⑲

⑫

⑯

⑳

Holders and Dispensers

Holders and dispensers help organize toiletries and other bathroom necessities. They're especially useful in bathrooms where space is limited. Storing items at the point of use makes routines easier.

Here are some simple suggestions:

- Choose holders that are easy to clean. Accessories that are permanently installed should have removable parts that can be hand-washed or cleaned in a dishwasher, especially toothbrush holders.

- Be careful about choosing glass accessories, particularly for bathrooms children will use. Unbreakable plastic is often a better choice.

- Wall-mounted accessories work well in bathrooms with limited counter space, such as those with pedestal or console sinks.

- Position toilet paper holders 8 to 12 inches (20 to 30 cm) in front of the toilet and 26 inches (66 cm) above the floor.

① This simple toothbrush holder and soap dish are small enough to be stored on the glass ledge between uses.

② Shiny chrome holders make even mundane items such as toilet paper and a toilet brush appear attractive.

③ A wall-mounted dispenser transforms a tissue holder into an accessory.

④ In a case of serious attention to detail, this ceramic soap dish echoes the shape of the wall-hung sink and toilet.

⑤ This beaker and soap dispenser repeat the use of stainless steel from the counter and backsplash to create a coordinated bathroom.

Holders and dispensers can be subjected to fairly heavy use, so it's important that they have high-quality finishes. Metals should resist tarnish, rust, and water spots. Rubber coatings should be thick but flexible enough to withstand daily use. Make sure any glass accessories are sturdy, and replace them at the first sign of cracks or chips.

Wall-mounted accessories are sold with the necessary hanging hardware. Make sure the hardware is attached to framing studs or use sturdy anchors to install it; without adequate support they can eventually become unstable.

① Bath rack
② Bar-soap dishes
③ Wall-mounted toothbrush holders
④ Pump dispensers for liquid soap, lotion, or hand sanitizer
⑤ Wall-mounted toilet roll holders
⑥ Toilet brush caddies

④

⑤

⑥

Hooks, Rings, and Bars

They may only be small conveniences, but they're details most of us appreciate. Who doesn't enjoy finding a clean, dry bath towel at hand when they step out of the shower or tub? Who isn't happy to find a hand towel beside the sink when they've washed their hands? Hooks, rings, and towel bars satisfy these needs.

Design authorities suggest bathrooms include:

- 24 inches (60 cm) of towel-bar space for each user of a bathroom.
- One towel hook or ring within 12 inches (30 cm) of a tub or shower.
- One robe hook for each bathroom user.

These accessories should be chosen in styles and finishes that coordinate with the room's faucets, fittings, and light fixtures. Although it's not necessary that they all match exactly, they should work together to advance the bathroom's design.

① Brushed-nickel bars and hooks keep towels and bathing accessories close to this small vanity.

② A clever, hinge-like mechanism allows this towel bar to swing into position when needed. When not in use, the bar folds neatly against the wall.

③ Hooks and cubbies keep belongings organized for the three users of this cheerful bathroom.

④ Towel rings work especially well in tight quarters, such as the small space between this sink and vanity.

⑤ A freestanding rack takes up only a few inches, but provides space to hang robes, towels, and clothes.

⑥ A train-rack-style shelf includes a bar for a towel in use and storage for several more.

⑦ A unique semi-circular holder grasps a rolled towel in this modern bath.

④

⑥

⑤

⑦

Single and double hooks are useful for robes as well as towels.

Towel rings are most often used to hold hand towels beside sinks. When hanging a towel ring, make sure there will be at least 18 inches (30 cm) of clear space for the towel to hang.

Towel bars are typically sold in 18- and 24-inch (30- and 60-cm) lengths. Most bathrooms benefit from a combination of these two sizes. In bathrooms used by adults, towel bars should hang 48 inches (120 cm) above the floor. Their height is lowered to 36 inches (90 cm) in children's bathrooms. Always be sure there is enough space below the bar for the towel to hang without covering electrical outlets.

① Robe hooks
② Towel rings
③ Towel bars

①

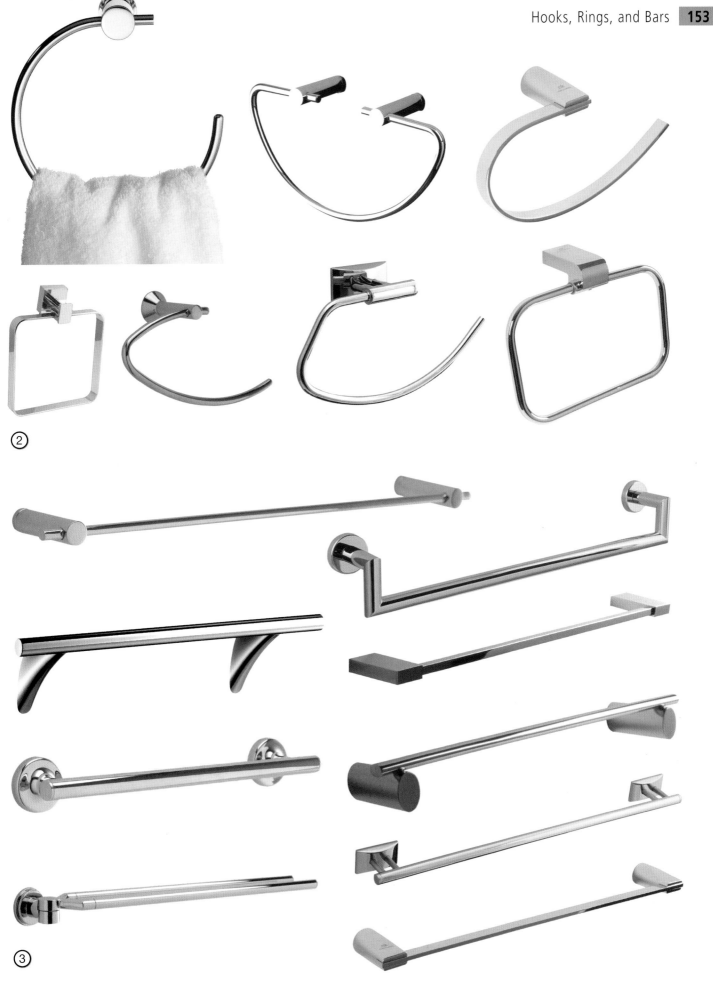

②

③

Mirrors

Mirrors have a decisive impact on a bathroom's appearance. As well as their practical uses, they can enhance the available light and make the room seem larger. They can also be used as artwork.

Mirrors should be chosen with the overall balance of the room in mind. Many cover the entire area behind a vanity, though individual mirrors have become popular in recent years and typically are approximately the same width as the sinks below them.

However it is employed in the design of a bathroom, a mirror must work for its users. To make it accessible, the center of the mirror should be hung at the eye level of the most frequent users. Good ventilation prevents fogging, but mirrors themselves are also available with de-fogging technology built in.

① A wide, frameless mirror hangs above the sink, illuminated by two wall sconces. Nearby, a framed, full-length mirror leans against the wall of the dressing area.

② Matching round, frameless mirrors are lovely counterpoints to the rectangular sinks below.

③ The glass frame of this mirror echoes the pattern of stripes etched into the vanity doors below. The frame reaches to the edges of the vanity, centering the mirror itself on the sink.

④ The baroque frame of this mirror repeats the theme of the wallpaper, both of which provide interesting contrast with the other, more simple, lines of the room.

⑤ In an unusual arrangement, a tiny mirror on a flexible stem reflects above a small sink.

Wall and Floor Finishes

Choosing bathroom wall and floor coverings is both an art and a science. As the largest surfaces in the room, the walls and floors set the stage aesthetically for the fixtures and fittings. They are, however, more than mere backgrounds. They define the size and shape of the room and play a large part in its success. On the practical side, well-chosen wall and floor coverings enhance a bathroom's safety and need to fulfill certain durability and maintenance requirements.

Let's face it: beneath their shiny and sometimes glamorous surfaces, bathrooms are practical, functional spaces. They're exposed to constant moisture, a fair share of dirt, and daily wear and tear. The true measure of success is whether they can stand up to all that and still look fresh a few years down the road. That's why it's important to choose wall and floor coverings that are resistant to water, easy to clean, and simple to maintain.

Bathrooms can be divided into two zones: wet and dry. Wet zones are the areas in close proximity to water sources—sinks, tubs, and showers. With wall coverings you can afford to be more flexible, depending on which zone you're dealing with. In dry zones (the areas that stay dry), you can be less practical, but the wall coverings in wet zones need to be water resistant as well as durable and attractive. When it comes to floor coverings, make sure you choose one that will serve both wet and dry zones. Not all flooring types can meet the needs of both. A floor surface that combines water- and slip-resistance is essential.

In this chapter we'll look at a variety of wall and floor coverings and discuss the advantages of these materials as well as any disadvantages. We'll take note of issues that separate high-quality versions from lesser quality products. We'll also point out reasons you might choose to splurge on a product and where you can save money without sacrificing style or quality.

As always, it's critical to match the materials to the ways the room will be used. The metallic floor that would be perfect for a guest bath might not be a very good choice for a family bath. The type of washable wallpaper you'd choose for a children's bath might be a little out of place in an elegant spa environment. But with the variety of materials available, you're sure to find the one that's right for your bathroom.

Opposite: Thousands of tiny mosaic tiles march in straight lines across the walls and floor of this bathroom. The stripes are created by nothing more than a series of shifts in color.

Below: Here's a simple but effective combination. The wood floors and wall warm up the white-on-white color scheme of the painted wall and fixtures.

Types, Styles, and Approaches

Choosing coverings for bathroom walls and floors is a matter of balancing form with function. It becomes a search for the look you want combined with the characteristics you need. The various care requirements may help you narrow the field of choices. Classic options include:

Ceramic, porcelain, and glass tile: Glass and glazed tiles require practically no maintenance. Seal grout periodically to maintain water resistance. Inspect frequently and replace cracked grout immediately.

Paint: Wash walls periodically.

Sheet vinyl and linoleum: Sweep often and mop periodically.

Natural stone: Some require little beyond sweeping and mopping. Others require careful maintenance. Investigate these characteristics before deciding on stone.

Wood: Maintain finish, as a worn finish will not resist water effectively.

Polished concrete: Fill substantial cracks and seal the surface once a year.

① In this bathroom, painted drywall covers the walls in dry zones, while hardwood protects a wet-zone wall and the floor.

② Here, painted drywall brightens the dry zone, but the wall behind the tub is tiled, as is the floor. As large tile has fewer grout lines to provide slip-resistance, it must have texture when used on floors to prevent accidents.

③ Sheet vinyl is inexpensive, easy to clean, and durable. It's also available in a variety of colors, patterns, and styles.

④ Cool and elegant, marble has been used as flooring for centuries. Tiles are more practical than slabs because individual pieces can be replaced if damaged. Superficial scratches can be buffed out by professionals.

⑤ Decorative inserts embellish this metal plank floor and add slip-resistance. Check for finishes that resist water spots.

⑥ Wallpaper designed for bathrooms is treated to be water resistant and durable, even in heavily used family baths.

Tiles

For bathroom wall and floor coverings, glazed ceramic and porcelain tile lead the pack. Both of these types of tile are made from clay pressed into shape and fired in kilns. When glazed, they are durable, water resistant, and can be quite colorful.

It can be difficult to tell the difference between ceramic and porcelain without looking at the label, but they are each colored using a different method.

Unglazed tile is porous and softer than glazed tile. It's rarely a good choice for a bathroom but can be used if sealed well and maintained.

Stone tile is the next most popular choice, but not all stone is equal. Some, such as granite, are impervious to water and resistant to chemicals. Others, such as marble, stain easily and require periodic sealing and careful maintenance.

① Limestone is hard and impervious to water—an excellent choice for bathrooms. Use large tiles, as on these walls, or tiny cubes, like those around the mirror.

② Tiny, metallic glass mosaic tiles adorn these shower walls, while large, black marble tile covers the wall behind the sink. The floor is clad in white marble.

③ Notice how the grout around these large, glazed ceramic tiles blends with the tile.

④ Large, textured porcelain tile covers these walls and slightly smaller tile covers the floor of the spa bath. Porcelain tile is often designed to mimic stone and it can be difficult to tell the difference between the two.

⑤ Two colors of ceramic tile set in a bold geometric pattern add plenty of style at virtually no additional cost.

⑥ By virtue of its many grout lines, a mosaic tile surface is slip-resistant as well as charming, so mosaic can be used for floors as well as walls.

Ceramic and porcelain wall tiles are not charged with supporting great weight, so they are generally thinner and less expensive than their floor equivalents.

Wall tiles are available in sizes ranging from 1-inch (2.5-cm) mosaic tiles to 16-inch (40-cm) squares. Modern subway tiles, measuring 3 x 6 inches (7.5 x 15 cm), are popular, as are standard 4-inch (10-cm) squares.

Ceramic tile gets its color from glazes that are fired onto its surface. In contrast, color is distributed throughout the body of a porcelain tile. Because the color runs all the way through porcelain tile, it can be molded to include realistic, stone-like textures, and it shows damage less easily.

① Stone effect in white ceramic
② Smooth tan ceramic
③ Smooth sage ceramic
④ Smooth pastel-blue ceramic
⑤ Smooth mustard ceramic
⑥ Smooth burgundy ceramic
⑦ Smooth plum ceramic
⑧ Smooth malachite ceramic
⑨ Speckled gray ceramic
⑩ Clouded tan ceramic
⑪ Speckled royal-blue ceramic
⑫ Speckled brown ceramic
⑬ Smooth ivory porcelain
⑭ Sponged beige porcelain
⑮ Veined cream porcelain
⑯ Marbled gray porcelain
⑰ Stone-effect, blue-gray porcelain
⑱ Veined tan and brown porcelain
⑲ Sponged gold porcelain
⑳ Brushed henna porcelain

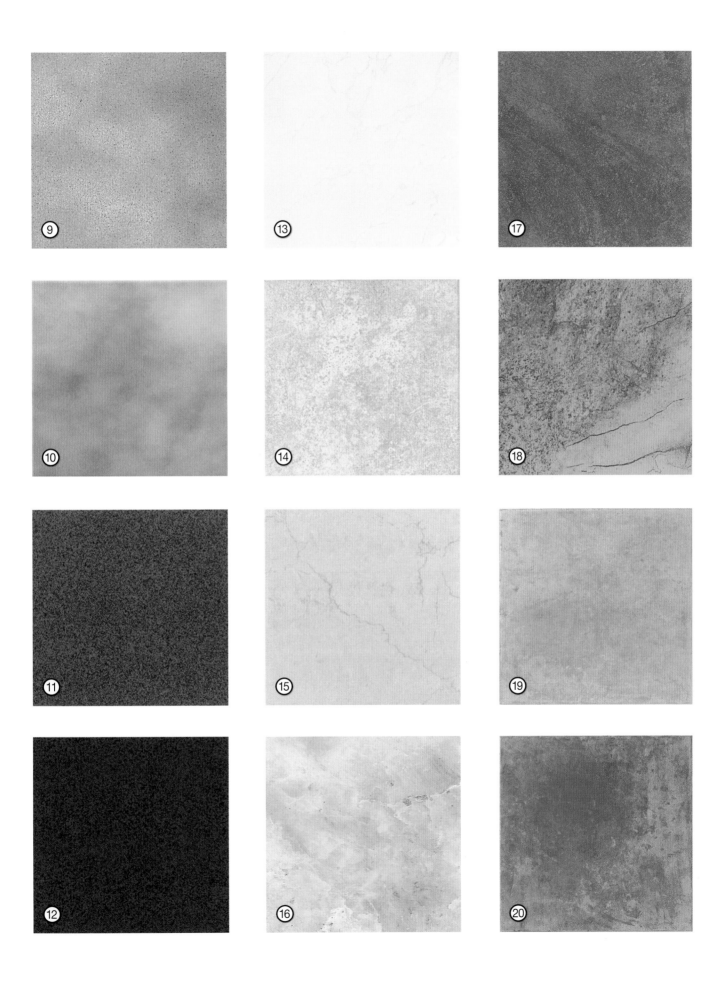

Ceramic and porcelain floor tile is designed to bear the weight of fixtures, furniture, and foot traffic. It is thicker and heavier than wall tile and can be used on countertops. Floor tile ranges in size from 1-inch (2.5-cm) mosaics to 16-inch (40-cm) squares, with 12-inch (30-cm) squares quite common.

When shopping for floor tile, check its slip-resistance. Many products carry "coefficient of friction" ratings to indicate their slip-resistance. The higher the coefficient, the more slip-resistant the tile. A dry coefficient of 0.6 is the minimum standard for the Americans with Disabilities Act, which is an excellent guide.

① Marbled pale gray ceramic
② Marbled taupe ceramic
③ Slate-effect copper ceramic
④ Rust-effect blue ceramic
⑤ Sponged mist ceramic
⑥ Slate-effect earth ceramic
⑦ Slate-effect aluminum ceramic
⑧ Sponged chalk ceramic
⑨ Stone-effect iron and olive porcelain
⑩ Stone-effect plum and tan porcelain
⑪ Stone-effect seashell porcelain
⑫ Streaked tan porcelain
⑬ Streaked wheat porcelain
⑭ Flecked tan porcelain
⑮ Granite-effect gravel porcelain
⑯ Granite-effect pebble porcelain
⑰ Smooth gray porcelain
⑱ Slate-effect sorrel porcelain
⑲ Slate-effect blue porcelain
⑳ Slate-effect deep-blue porcelain

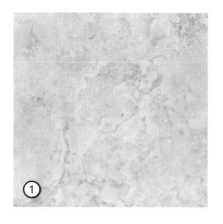

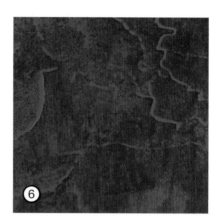

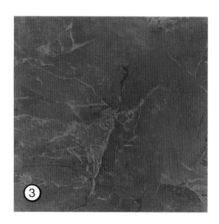

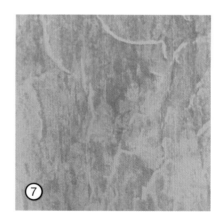

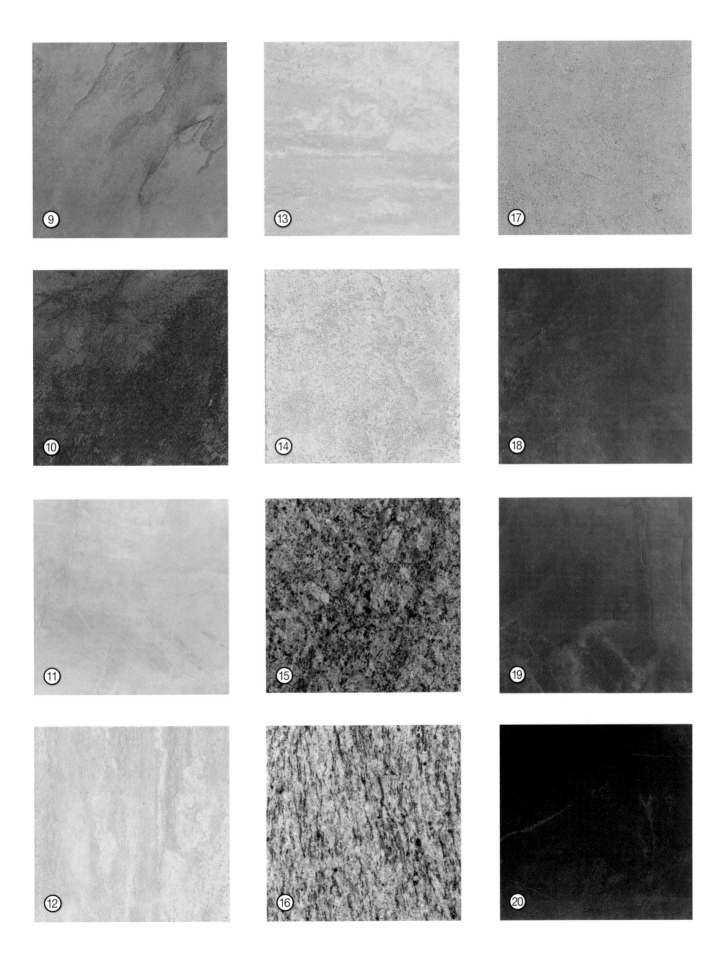

Some varieties of stone are more suited to bathrooms than others.

Limestone is a sedimentary stone. It is hard, impervious to water, and has a fine to very fine grain.

Marble is a dense form of limestone transformed through heat and pressure.

Slate is a fine-grained stone that is easily split into layers. It tends to be softer and more porous than most stone. Slate has to be sealed periodically and maintained carefully in bathrooms.

Travertine is a hard, sedimentary stone deposited from the water of mineral springs. Unfilled, its surface has many holes and troughs, which can be protected with a clear, epoxy resin. Filled and polished, it has a smooth, shiny surface.

① Frosted antique white limestone
② Brushed brown limestone
③ Cream polished limestone
④ Brushed silver limestone
⑤ Polished, veined white marble
⑥ Polished Italian-beige marble
⑦ Polished deep-brown marble
⑧ Polished Inca-gold marble
⑨ Polished black marble
⑩ Polished beige and ivory marble
⑪ Polished cherry-blossom marble
⑫ Polished terra-cotta marble
⑬ Amazon-green slate
⑭ Rustic multicolor slate
⑮ Filled, light-tan and gray travertine
⑯ Honed, clouded cream travertine
⑰ Unfilled coral travertine
⑱ Honed, filled light-walnut travertine
⑲ Honed, filled gold travertine
⑳ Unfilled, dark-walnut travertine

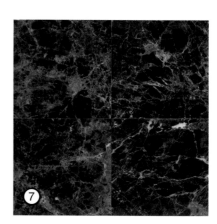

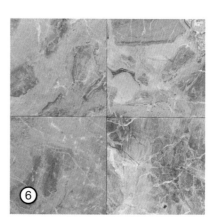

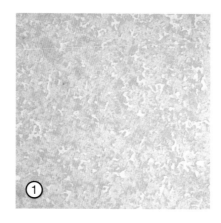

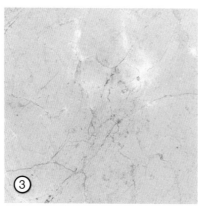

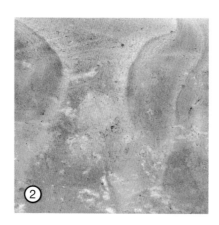

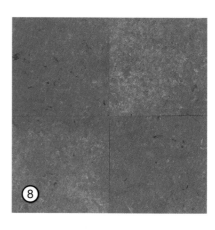

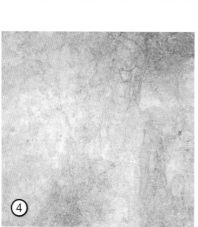

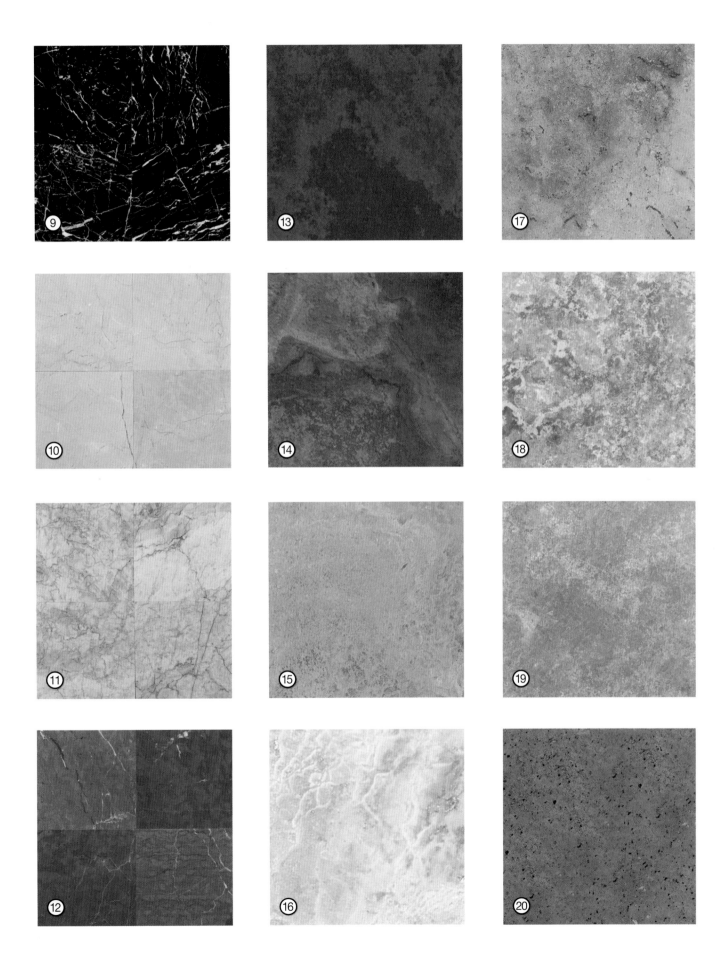

Mosaic tile is an excellent choice for bathroom floors. It's easy to install and the multitude of grout lines makes it extremely slip-resistant. On walls, it offers limitless decorative options.

From ancient times until today, artists have created incredible mosaics using tiny pieces of tile. It's no longer necessary to be an artist to work with mosaics. These days, individual tiles are mounted on a mesh backing that lets you install dozens of tiles at one time.

Ceramic, porcelain, terra-cotta, and stone are commonly cut into mosaic tile. Most mosaics require very little maintenance, though terra-cotta products have to be sealed periodically.

1. Loose sheet of stone
2. Loose sheet of chalk
3. Loose sheet of straw
4. Loose sheet of brick
5. Grouted coffee and cream
6. Grouted shades of brown
7. Grouted shades of blue and white
8. Grouted white in two sizes
9. Grouted classic checkerboard
10. Grouted white around black
11. Grouted gray and white with wide joints
12. Grouted gold and white with wide joints
13. Grouted chalk
14. Grouted lemon
15. Grouted sunlit gray
16. Grouted mottled tan
17. Grouted tan hexagons and diamonds
18. Grouted gray hexagons and diamonds
19. Grouted contrasting diamonds
20. Grouted aqua gray with wide joints

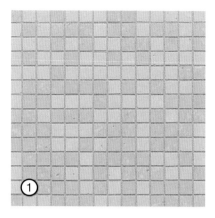

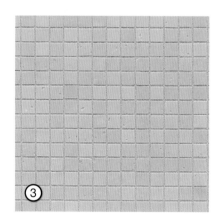

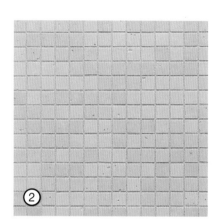

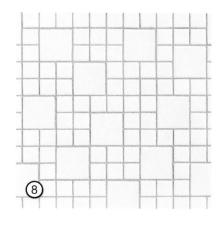

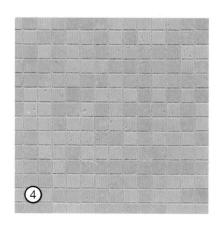

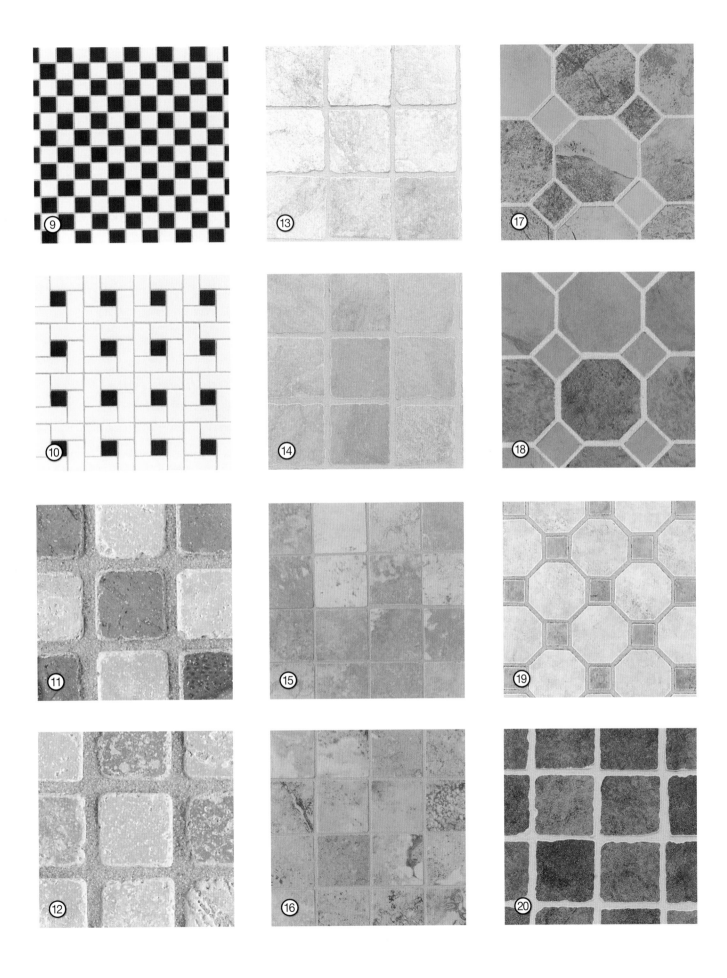

Glass tiles are impervious to water and stains and resistant to discoloration and damage from chemicals. They are, however, more susceptible to cracks and chips than many other tile types. Surface preparation is critical in glass tile installations because any damage can be seen. When installing glass tile over load-bearing walls or other structures prone to settling, use an anti-fracture membrane.

Metal tiles are an interesting alternative. They are available with smooth, polished, and unpolished finishes, and with embossed designs. Some metals weather and discolor over time if they're exposed to moisture, so bear this in mind when making your selection.

① Translucent glass
② Translucent glass in ice-blue
③ Stone-effect frost
④ Stone-effect glass in crimson
⑤ Petroleum-effect glass in pearl
⑥ Petroleum-effect glass in gold
⑦ Etched tile in apricot
⑧ Stone-effect glass in gray-green
⑨ Etched glass in blue pearl
⑩ Etched glass in jade
⑪ Etched glass in cherry
⑫ Etched glass in petroleum black
⑬ Satin mat metal in silver
⑭ Satin mat metal in bright gold
⑮ Satin mat metal in dark bronze
⑯ Satin mat metal in orange-red
⑰ Floral design metal in blue
⑱ Abstract design on aqua metal
⑲ Cross design on gold metal
⑳ Swirled design on silver metal

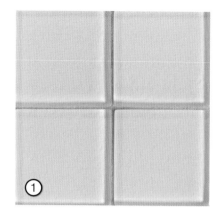

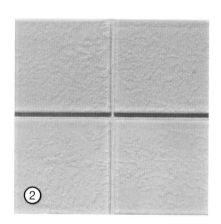
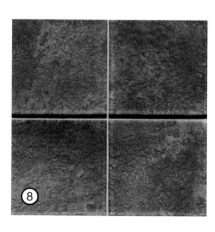
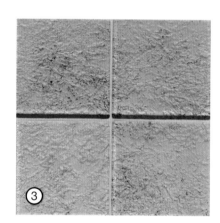

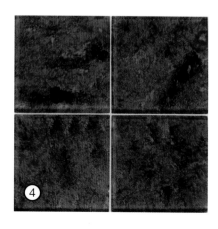
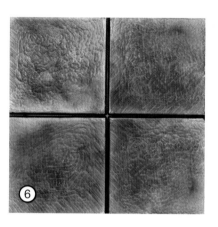

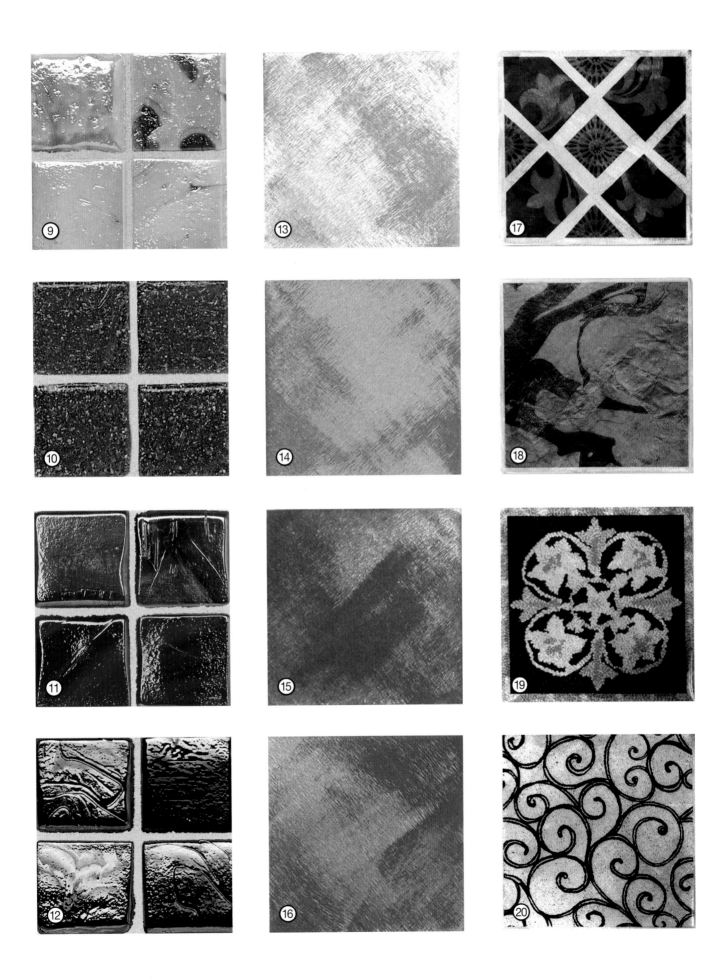

Tile Murals

A tile mural transforms a bathroom wall into an artistic statement unlike any other. Many murals are custom-designed for the space and created by artists who hand-apply individual tiles to the wall itself or to mesh backing for later installation.

If an artist's mosaic is beyond your budget, don't despair. Many companies produce less costly versions, some based on photographs supplied by the customer. Computer software translates the image into a master plan, which the craftsperson is then able to follow in much the same way one would follow a needlepoint or cross-stitch chart. The finished pieces are stunning.

Some manufacturers and artists offer hand-painted murals created on larger tile.

① Individual black and white mosaic tiles are combined to create the intricate detail of this image.

② A colorful mosaic-tile mermaid floats in a sea of blue tile, lit by a skylight.

③ Hand-painted tile makes up a lighthouse mural tucked into an unusual space in this New England-style home.

④ This mural was created through a special process that translates a large photograph into a series of tile-sized images. The individual images are then reproduced, each on its own tile.

⑤ Stylized animals stampede across the center of this shower wall. Graphic designs like this make extremely effective use of a relatively small number of decorative tiles.

Combining Tiles to Make Patterns

Imagination and creativity can often accomplish what even huge outlays of money may not: unique designs customized to your personal taste. With some time and consideration, you can develop a layout that produces striking effects with nothing more than variations in color placement and, perhaps, size. For a subtle effect, try a tone-on-tone pattern that alternates between glossy and mat finishes.

When designing a pattern, consider the size of the room in relationship to the scale of the pattern. Large patterns often require large spaces, while small patterns tend to run together in large spaces. This is not universally true, however, so don't be afraid to try unusual combinations in the experimental stages of the project.

Alternating checkerboard

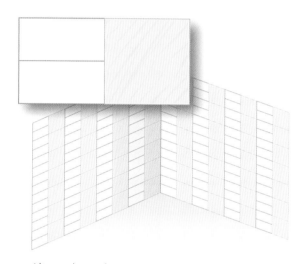

Alternating strips

Standard checkerboard

Herringbone

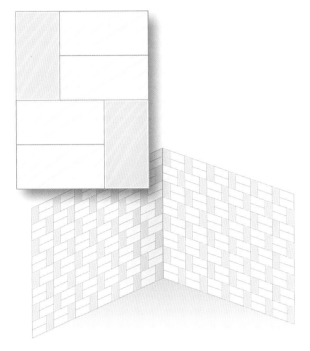

Basketweave variation

Running bond with alternating brick colors

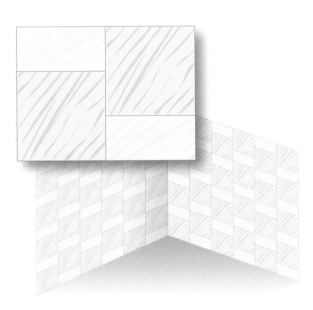

Barred square

Railroad bond

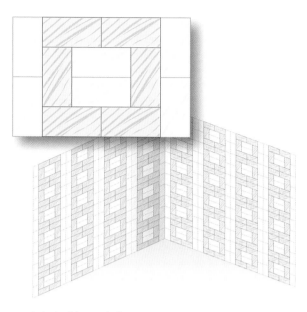

Interlocking spiral

Pinwheel

Block pattern with random square border

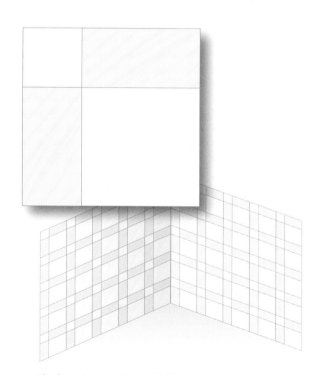

Block pattern with inlaid block border

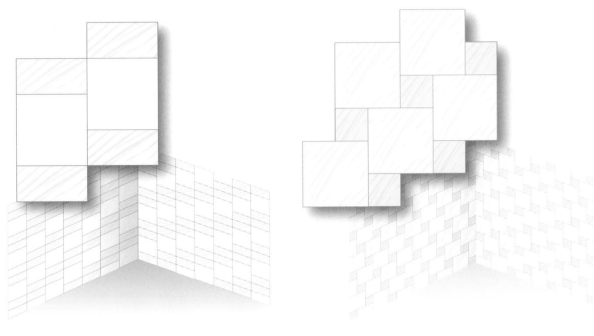

Diagonal stripe

Diagonal variation

Diagonal block

Diagonal

Paint and Wallpaper

Other wall finishes may get more attention, but for ease of application and maintenance, durability, and affordability, it would be hard to beat paint or wallpaper.

The appearance of a painted wall doesn't start with paint, it starts with drywall (known as "greenboard") designed to withstand moisture. Walls must be carefully repaired and prepared before they are painted.

The best paint finish for a frequently used bathroom is semi-gloss. Eggshell is acceptable in a guest bath, but generally speaking, the shinier the paint, the better it withstands moisture. If you don't like the shine of semi-gloss, look for paint labeled washable. It's specifically manufactured to be exposed to water. Some manufacturers also offer paint specially formulated to prevent the growth of mold and mildew.

After a decade of being out of favor, wallpaper is making a comeback. With reasonably priced laser levels readily available, hanging wallpaper is no longer a huge challenge. Most modern wallpapers—with the possible exception of flocked papers—will stand up to the humid conditions of a bathroom.

① Charcoal-gray walls and a nearly-black floor allow white fixtures to sparkle in this unique room.

② These walls take their color cue from the mosaic tile of the shower. It's always a good idea to match the paint color to another element of the room.

③ A deep-red wall separates the vanity area from the bathing and toilet areas in this modest bathroom.

④ The curved lines of this contemporary, black and white wallpaper print make a great foil for the straight lines of some of the fixtures and fittings.

⑤ The strong vertical lines of this luxuriant wallpaper provide balance for the horizontal line of the square tub and double vanity.

⑥ In a historic or reproduction home, period wallpaper creates atmosphere as long as it's faithful to the era.

Wood

The warmth of wood can be an antidote to the sometimes clinical feel of a bathroom. Wood not only looks warm, it feels warm to the touch. It's also durable and easy to clean. However, in order to retain their good looks, wood walls and floors must be properly sealed and maintained.

Tongue-and-groove paneling, sometimes called beadboard, is a favorite for bathroom walls. It's typically sold in 3- to 5-inch (7.5- to 12.5-cm) wide pieces designed to fit together. Wood flooring is sold in a variety of styles—in 2¼-inch (5.5-cm) strips, 5-inch (12.5-cm) planks, and mosaic pieces called parquet.

Engineered wood products—paneling as well as flooring—consist of several layers of wood pressed together. Research engineered wood carefully before you buy: some inexpensive products delaminate when exposed to water.

① Hardwood planks on the wall to the left emphasize the length of this rectangular bathroom. Solid surface material and wallpaper are used on the walls in the wet zones.

② Reclaimed wood offers unique shading and characteristics. Here the glow of vintage wood makes a beautiful counterpoint to modern fixtures.

③ Beautiful grain patterns highlight the walls and floors of this room. A smoked-glass panel separates the vanity area from the toilet and bidet without disrupting the room's flow.

④ Paint helps any wood stand up to the conditions of a bathroom. Exterior floor paint, particularly the type manufactured for porch floors, is exceptionally durable.

⑤ Wide, honey-colored planks repeat the color and shape of the wood counters in this soothing retreat.

⑥ Carved wood panels protected by black paint make a stunning statement here. The carving's relief creates fascinating shadows and textures that echo the trees outside the window.

Wood varieties each have their own unique characteristics and colors. Colors can be enhanced with stain, but nothing can replicate the unique appearance of, for example, bird's-eye maple or burled oak. The samples shown here will help you get an idea of the type of wood that appeals to you most.

Please think about sustainability when you shop for wood. It's true that wood is a renewable resource, but it's also true that irresponsible harvesting practices have the potential to damage forests, especially when it comes to exotic woods. If sustainability concerns you, look for the logo of The Forest Stewardship Council. It ensures the wood you purchase was grown and harvested responsibly.

① Acacia
② Andiroba
③ Ash
④ Beech
⑤ Bamboo
⑥ Birch
⑦ Amboyna burl
⑧ Cherry
⑨ Hickory
⑩ Jarrah
⑪ Jatobá
⑫ Mahogany
⑬ Oak
⑭ Maple
⑮ Merbau
⑯ African padauk
⑰ Pine
⑱ Rosewood
⑲ Sapele
⑳ Walnut

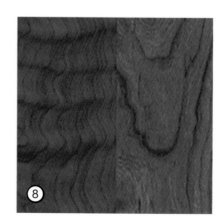

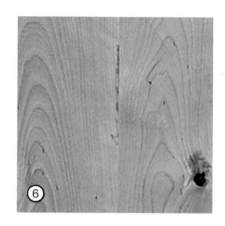

Resilient Flooring

Resilient flooring is a term that includes vinyl tiles and sheet vinyl as well as linoleum. The word "resilient" refers to the tendency of these products to cushion your footsteps. All three types wear well, resist water, and clean up easily.

Resilient flooring, especially sheet vinyl, is very common in children's and family baths. Most of these products are reasonably priced and cost effective. Plus, you don't have to do anything but sweep and damp-mop them from time to time.

Installing resilient flooring is a realistic do-it-yourself project for someone with the time and patience for it. The most challenging part of the process is producing an accurate template for cutting the flooring.

① This sheet-vinyl floor, which mimics the look of a cobblestone street, fits in with the traditional, wood-paneled walls and carved trim.

② Black-and-white checkerboard linoleum never goes out of style, especially for traditional bathrooms like this.

③ The terra-cotta background and sprightly dots of the linoleum blend establish a neutral foundation for this bathroom. The wood mat in the center reinforces the natural, fresh atmosphere.

④ Sheet vinyl replicates many natural materials—here, wood is the inspiration.

Linoleum flooring is an all-organic laminate consisting of a layer of linseed oil, wood flour, pine resin, and mineral pigments bonded to a jute backing. It is a good choice for allergy suffers and chemically sensitive people.

These samples will give you a taste of the many patterns and styles available.

① Range of colors in marble finish
② Geometric pattern
③ Simple border
④ Faux tiles in copper
⑤ Faux marble
⑥ Faux tiles with inlay
⑦ Faux granite
⑧ Faux blue marble
⑨ Spattered effect
⑩ Faux tiles in aged brown
⑪ Faux oak
⑫ Faux tiles in burnished blue
⑬ Faux metal tiles with insets
⑭ Faux stone parquet
⑮ Faux walnut
⑯ Faux craggy paving
⑰ Faux mosaic tiles in gold
⑱ Faux mosaic tiles in moss
⑲ Faux beech
⑳ Faux glass
㉑ Faux mosaic tiles in chocolate

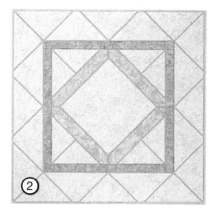

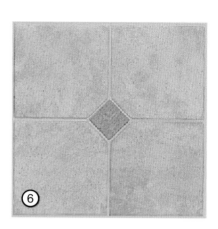

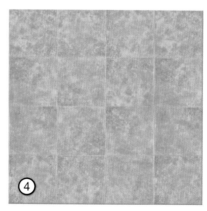

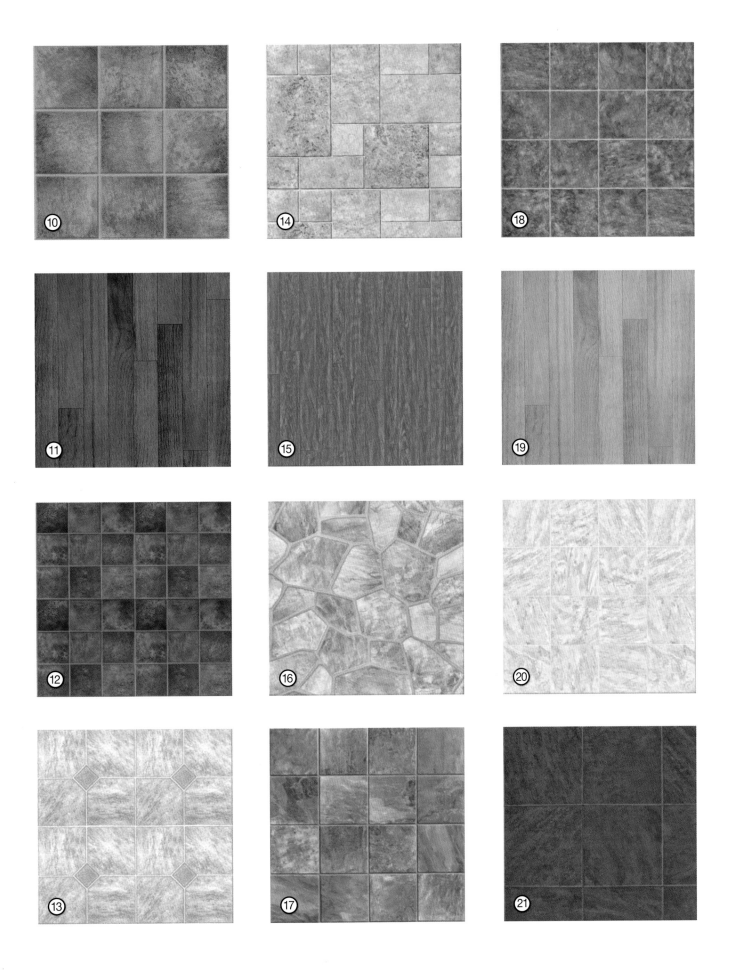

Vinyl flooring is produced by transforming vinyl chips into solid sheets through the application of heat and pressure. It is sold in two styles: perimeter bond and full bond. The adhesive is spread only at the edges and seams of perimeter-bond flooring; adhesive is spread across the entire work area for full-bonded flooring.

It's possible to install a new layer of vinyl flooring directly over an old layer, as long as only one layer is present. To check, pull out a heat register or other fixed object in the room and look at the cut edges of the hole.

The popularity of vinyl flooring is at least partly the result of the wide range of colors, patterns, and styles to choose from. Here are some samples of what's available.

① Faux terrazzo, light
② Faux terrazzo, dark
③ Faux limestone
④ Faux rough plaster
⑤ Checkerboard pattern
⑥ Geometric pattern
⑦ Faux white marble
⑧ Faux tiles in sky effect
⑨ Flowerbud pattern in mottled finish
⑩ Autumnal leaf pattern
⑪ Faux bamboo shoots
⑫ Faux black slate
⑬ Faux exotic wood
⑭ Faux birch
⑮ Faux mahogany
⑯ Faux oak
⑰ Dot pattern
⑱ Faux glass mosaic
⑲ Faux brick
⑳ Faux wooden inlay

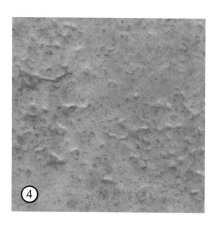

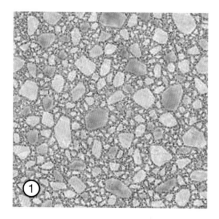

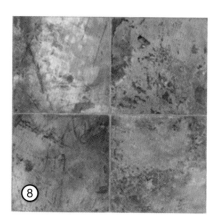

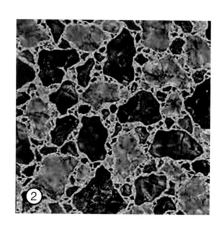

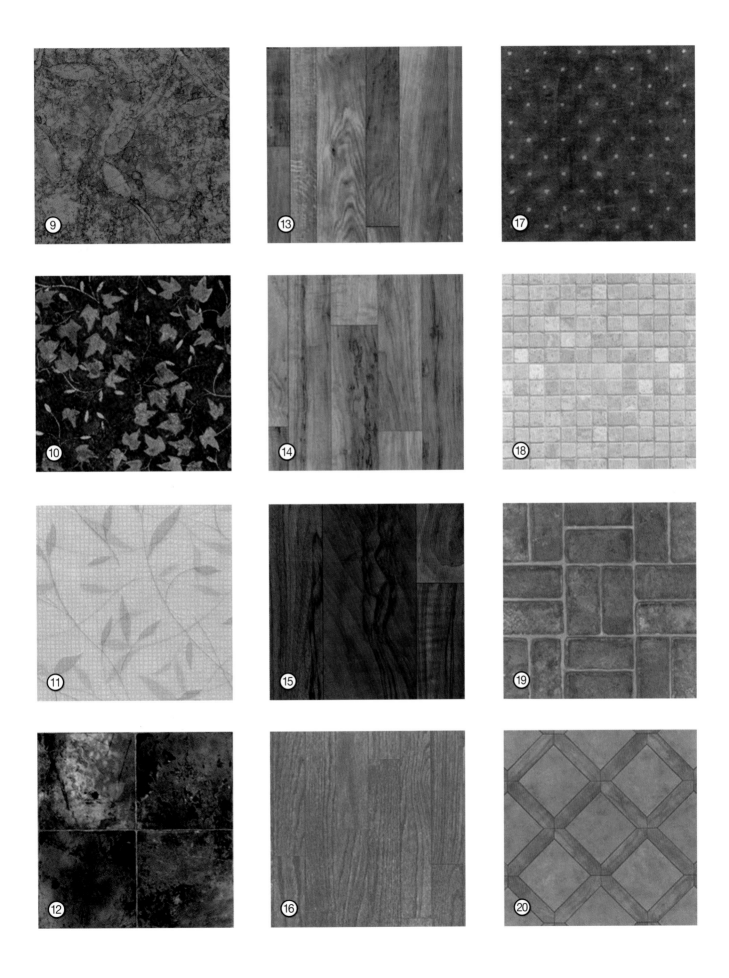

Using Color

Use the color of the floors and walls to set the palette for a bathroom. Fixtures are more difficult and expensive to replace, and trends change quickly. Nothing screams "I'm from the 80s" louder than a burgundy toilet.

Many people try to avoid this problem by forgoing color altogether. Neutral colors certainly have a place in bathrooms, but restricting yourself to them means you miss the opportunity to create a mood for the room.

① The soft colors of the garden and the sky will gently wake you up. This is a room that would add cheer to even the gloomiest day.

② Color experts often use green as a neutral. Combining leafy greens with the colors of water and earth brings the outdoors in.

③ Honey-colored walls spiced up with red cabinets create a mellow glow, to calm you even after the busiest day.

④ Mixing robin's-egg blue with chocolate brown produces a warm, serene room that's a pleasure to return to.

⑤ Neutral grays and whites produce a plain, but calming room.

⑥ Warm colors like these offer cheerful comfort, which is sure to be welcome in any weather.

⑦ Black and white is a classic combination that never goes out of style. Adding an accent color, such as this bright pink, creates energy.

⑧ Spicy colors create a room that's warm and cozy, but will still send you out into the day filled with pep and excitement.

Heating and Ventilation

Few things spoil a long, hot shower or bath like stepping out into a cold, damp room. Even in homes with central heating and otherwise good ventilation, bathrooms can become uncomfortably cool on winter days and the air can feel damp or smell less than fresh. Supplemental sources of heat and ventilation resolve this issue. Ventilation is more than a matter of comfort, though. It can affect the condition of a house as well as the health of its inhabitants.

Opposite: A white radiator stands within a gleaming towel warmer designed for traditional-style bathrooms.

Below: An exhaust fan provides ventilation and a slim, multi-rack towel warmer supplies gentle warmth in this toilet area.

The most common type of supplemental heat for bathrooms is radiant heat. This kind of heat, which can be quite cost effective, produces no chemicals, dust particles, odors, or fumes. Typically, radiant heat is provided through floor-warming systems (low-voltage mesh mats) or individual radiators.

Radiators transfer heat to the coldest objects in a room first, typically the floor and fixtures. It is this property that makes radiators so popular in bathrooms. After all, who wouldn't welcome warm floors and fixtures on a cold day? Despite being efficient sources of heat, radiators don't get hot enough to cause burns. And, when protected by ground fault circuit interrupters and placed at proper distances, they can be safely used around water sources.

From the comfort and luxury of warm floors and fixtures, it's only a small step to warm towels. Many manufacturers offer products that provide supplemental heat as well as warm towels and generate gentle heat for drying delicate clothing. And there's no reason to hide them away.

Today's radiators and towel warmers are designed to be as attractive as they are efficient.

When it comes to bathroom ventilation, exhaust fans are the answer. They provide fresh air while carrying away moisture and odors. A hot shower or bath can elevate a bathroom's humidity level to 100 percent in only a few minutes. The result can be foggy mirrors and condensation on walls and windows. An exhaust fan removes excess humidity, which protects wall and window coverings and prevents the development of mold and mildew on surfaces throughout the room.

Not even the most efficient fan does any good unless you run it. In surveys, the most common reason given for not running bathroom fans is the noise level. Manufacturers have responded by developing quiet, smooth-running fans. Fan noise is measured in units known as sones. A fan with a sone rating of 1 can barely be heard when running. If you're sensitive to this kind of noise, choose a fan with a sone rating below 3.

Types, Styles, and Finishes

Supplemental heat sources for bathrooms include floor-warming systems, radiators, and gas or electric fireplaces.

Radiators and towel warmers force energy through a conductive material, such as metal, ceramic, or glass, to create resistance (heat). The heat then radiates out to cold surfaces in the room. Most are controlled by thermostats or remote controls.

Fireplaces are finding their way into bathrooms in record numbers. Most are sealed gas or electric units that can be operated by a wall switch or remote control.

Floor-warming systems comprise a low-voltage mesh mat and thermostat. They can be embedded in concrete or placed on top of the subfloor, beneath a tile or stone floor. They are then hard-wired into the bathroom's electrical system.

Exhaust fans are simple fans that provide ventilation and must be vented to the outside. They are controlled by wall switches.

(5)

① Chrome and cast iron work together in this hard-wired towel warmer/radiator combination.

② A sealed gas fireplace warms the atmosphere as well as the air surrounding this elegant tub.

③ Tucked beneath the vanity, this radiator puts warmth near the floor and allows it to rise into the room.

④ A simple towel warmer keeps towels toasty as it radiates warmth into the vanity area.

⑤ An exhaust fan is installed on the wall above this toilet. Fans must be high on the wall or in the ceiling to work effectively.

(6)

⑥ Hidden beneath the concrete floor, the mesh mat of a floor-warming system radiates heat into the room.

⑦ A wood shelf tops a traditional radiator in a bathroom filled with energy-efficient windows.

(7)

Radiators and Towel Warmers

Radiators typically are placed as near to the bathtub or shower as regulations allow. This creates a warm, comfortable environment for stepping out of the bath. Several types of radiators are widely available.

Metal radiators have rust-resistant finishes. Oil- and water-filled metal units cycle on and off, allowing the warm oil or water to radiate heat.

Ceramic radiators are considered especially appropriate for people who are chemically sensitive, as they produce virtually no fumes.

Glass radiators contain elements that transfer energy to the glass, which radiates warmth into the room.

Towel warmers are stylized units that provide radiant heat similar to that of a radiator, but they're designed to hold towels and other cloths.

②

①

③

① A glass radiator creates a cozy atmosphere right outside this glass shower.

② A gleaming two-rail chrome warmer mounted to the back of the bathing alcove keeps towels within easy reach of bathers.

③ A traditional radiator is topped by two towel-warmer rails in an attractive and efficient unit.

④ A ladder-style, wall-mounted unit could warm enough towels for a whole family to use.

⑤ A floor-mounted unit works beautifully next to this claw-foot tub.

⑥ Towels slip into the slots of this towel-warming tower, which can hold an extravagant supply of towels at one time.

Radiators and towel warmers

are available in styles ranging from traditional to contemporary. They are typically hard-wired into the bathroom's electrical system and controlled by a timer, thermostat, or remote control.

Towel warmers are a type of radiator. They slowly radiate warmth that heats towels and dries delicate laundry. Wall-mounted units make good use of space, but not every bathroom has a good place to install one. Floor-mounted units typically offer multiple rungs and exceptional capacity in family baths or other bathrooms shared by several users.

① Simple wall-mounted, two-rail chrome towel warmer
② Wall-mounted towel-warming shelf
③ Contemporary towel-warming shelf with bar
④ Traditional multiple-rail towel warmer
⑤ Art Deco wall-mounted towel warmer
⑥ Floor-mounted radiator with chrome towel warmer
⑦ Curved, cross-over radiator with multiple rails
⑧ Ladder-style towel warmer
⑨ Floor-mounted towel warmer
⑩ Ladder-style towel warmer
⑪ Radiator with multiple chrome towel-warmer rails
⑫ Space-saving chrome radiator
⑬ Curved chrome radiator
⑭ Tall, floor-mounted towel warmer with multiple rails

Exhaust Fans

Exhaust fans remove odors and excess moisture as well as provide fresh air. The Home Ventilating Institute suggests using an exhaust fan that provides a minimum of eight complete changes of air per hour in a bathroom.

Fans are sized according to the volume of air they can move per minute: cubic feet per minute, or CFM. The size of fan required increases as the volume of the room increases, as well as the number and size of fixtures in it. For example, a bathroom that includes a steam room requires more substantial ventilation than one with a small, standard shower. Consult your contractor or building-supply retailer for further information.

For maximum efficiency without wasting energy, exhaust fans should be run for no more than 20 minutes after a shower or bath.

① This unobtrusive, round exhaust fan is centrally located in the ceiling, between the tub and vanity areas.

② A square exhaust fan installed directly above the toilet works well in small areas such as this.

③ A small, square exhaust fan is mounted in the ceiling above this traditional tub.

④ The chandelier in this lovely room made installing an exhaust fan in the ceiling impractical. Instead, it was mounted as high as possible on the wall behind the toilet.

⑤ This high-tech fan is mounted on the wall of a multi-head shower. When the fan is in use, its iris opens to exhaust moisture.

⑥ With its iris closed, the exhaust fan is sealed, which prevents the loss of conditioned air.

Lighting

Let's face it: life is simply too short to look at ourselves in bad lighting. In flattering light, you (and the bathroom) look better. Bathrooms almost always include mirrors, often large ones, and these need to be well lit to be flattering and to let you see what you're doing when combing your hair or checking your clothes for lint. Aside from practical considerations, clever lighting is also an important design feature that can help your bathroom look its best.

Opposite: A dramatic interplay of illumination is created with a minimal amount of lighting for the vanity area of this contemporary bathroom.

Below: An elegant crystal and brass chandelier provides both light and dramatic style above this freestanding bathtub. A floor-to-ceiling window contributes light as well as a gorgeous view.

Good lighting doesn't just happen—it requires a plan. More complex lighting plans that involve illumination from a number of sources—what designers call "layers" of light—give greater flexibility. These layers may include natural and artificial light sources supplied at a variety of heights and from a variety of directions: up, down, and from the side.

Well-lit bathrooms are safer. By the age of 55, the average person's eyes require twice as much light for clear vision as they did when that same person was 20 years old. It makes sense to plan for the future as well as today when it comes to providing enough light. Lights should be positioned to reveal thresholds, steps, and areas that might be wet or slippery. Take note of the following points when planning your lighting.

With comfort in mind, whenever possible, natural light should contribute at least 10 percent of a room's general light. Frosted light bulbs produce less glare than clear bulbs, and shades soften the light from any type of bulb.

Skin tones look best in the warm light cast by incandescent bulbs or fluorescent bulbs with color temperatures of 3500K or less. Lights above mirrors cast unflattering shadows on faces if they're the only light sources in the area. Providing additional light from the sides balances the light levels and reduces those shadows.

Dimmers allow you to soften light levels to suit the time of day. Dimmers with a "slow start" feature slowly raise the light level over the course of a few seconds, which allows your eyes to adjust. This feature is especially valuable for nighttime visits to the bathroom.

As a shortcut, mirrors can be used to bounce light around a room, enhancing its effect. Placing a mirror on a wall opposite a window multiplies the light available to the room during the day.

Always make sure any electricity in your bathroom is installed safely. Lights located above bathtubs or within shower enclosures should be vapor-proof and clearly approved for use in wet locations.

Types and Styles

Successful lighting plans comprise a combination of ambient, task, accent, and decorative lighting.

Ambient lighting is the main layer of light in a room. It is provided by ceiling or wall-mounted fixtures as well as natural sources, such as windows and skylights.

Accent lighting highlights objects and adds depth and shade to the room. Lighted toekicks, uplight cans, and picture-frame lights are examples of this layer.

Task lighting provides illumination for specific purposes, such as lighting a vanity or bathing area or a shower.

Decorative lighting supplies light for the ambient layer, but its main purpose is to draw attention to fixtures themselves, such as sconces and chandeliers.

① Low-voltage pin lights gently light the ceiling of this appealing room.

② Pendant lamps hang to one side of the mirror, and lamps rest on a vanity below, providing task lighting for the room. (Lamps used in bathrooms must be plugged into GFCI-protected receptacles.)

③ A color-correct fluorescent fixture above the mirror provides task light for this vanity area.

④ Under-cabinet accent lights highlight the striking counters and backsplashes of this contemporary bathroom.

⑤ Sconces placed at eye level on either side of this mirror provide excellent task lighting. Uplights behind the cornice board add accent lighting.

⑥ Low-voltage track lights supply task lighting and a unique fluorescent chandelier adds decorative lighting to the plan.

⑦ Light glows around the edges of a partition wall behind a generous tub in a fine example of how effective accent lighting can be.

Ambient Lighting

Ambient lighting should include about one watt of incandescent light per square foot—two watts if the bulbs are recessed. When using fluorescent fixtures, provide one watt for every two to three square feet (0.2 to 0.3 square meters).

Incandescent, fluorescent, and halogen fixtures in the ceiling and walls provide the majority of the ambient light in most bathrooms.

Incandescent fixtures provide warm, yellowish light. The bulbs are inexpensive and readily available, but they're less energy efficient than other halogen or fluorescent bulbs.

Halogen fixtures provide pure, white light. Low-voltage bulbs are available in appealing sizes and shapes. They are energy efficient, but replacement bulbs tend to be expensive.

Fluorescent lights are energy efficient and economical. Color-corrected bulbs provide flattering light. Compact fluorescent bulbs, or CFLs, look like standard bulbs, but they last much, much longer. Fluorescent bulbs cannot be used with dimmers.

① Recessed halogen lights sparkle against the dark color of the ceiling and walls of this bathroom.

② Large recessed spotlights supply dramatic light for this room. Combined with the abundant natural light and the accent lighting on the vanity wall, they create an appealing lighting plan.

③ Two recessed lights highlight this shower area. Fixtures used in wet areas, such as shower enclosures, must be approved for this use.

④ A soffit above the vanity houses recessed fixtures as well as soft accent lighting directed toward the ceiling.

⑤ A brilliant collection of downlights and uplights creates reflections on the glossy tile surfaces of this bathroom, including the ceiling.

⑥ Low-voltage track lighting has been directed to provide ideal illumination for this room.

Accent Lighting

Wall fixtures and sconces offer excellent sources of accent and task lighting for bathrooms. Most sconces include some type of shade—either fabric, frosted glass, or ceramic—that reduces glare and adds decorative flair.

Wall sconces should be installed so the center of the fixture is at eye level. The mounting height varies slightly, depending on the style of the fixture and height of the ceiling, but most are centered about 66 inches (1.7 m) above the finished floor. Placing two sconces side by side provides cross-illumination that reduces shadows and diffuses soft light into the room.

① Brass sconces with frosted-glass shades provide excellent, low-glare task light for this vanity mirror.

② Swing arms allow users to adjust these lovely sconces as the task requires. The fabric shades soften the light and reduce shadows and glare in the mirror.

③ The light of this graceful chrome and glass sconce is reflected and multiplied by the glass shower enclosure.

④ Pairs of electric candle sconces on each side of the mirror provide a sense of elegance as well as cross-illumination for this vanity area.

⑤ Installing three fluorescent sconces on this wall provides even task lighting for the dual mirrors and vanity area.

⑥ A single, wide fluorescent fixture supplies task lighting for this vanity area. Under-mount lights provide accent lighting to the unique cabinets beyond.

Sconces and uplights work to create a warm glow in a bathroom. Choose them as carefully and with as much attention to their style and details as any other element of the bathroom, including fixtures and fittings.

Bronze, nickel, brass, antique brass, chrome, and vintage glass are common materials for bathroom light fixtures.

① Brass and crystal wall fixture
② Electric candle with brass finish and pleated shade
③ Contemporary wall sconce
④ Fluorescent picture-frame fixture
⑤ Small sconce with antique-brass finish and frosted-glass shade
⑥ Chrome and frosted-glass wall fixture.
⑦ Frosted-glass wall fixture
⑧ Chrome, dual-bulb wall fixture
⑨ Contemporary chrome fixture with frosted-glass shade
⑩ Square, frosted-glass sconce
⑪ Portal-style wall fixture with frosted-glass shade
⑫ Art Deco chrome fixture with frosted, egg-shaped shade
⑬ Ultra-contemporary glass and chrome wall fixture
⑭ Art Deco sconce with chrome details and frosted-glass shade
⑮ Candelabra-style wall fixture with fabric shades
⑯ Contemporary wall fixture with brushed-metal finish
⑰ Paintable bisque wall sconce
⑱ Mission-style chrome downlight with frosted-glass shade
⑲ Gooseneck fixture with wood grain and antique-bronze finishes
⑳ Traditional-style sconce with polished-nickel finish and frosted-glass shade

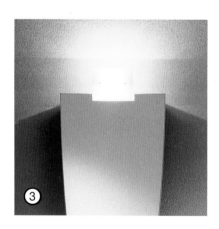

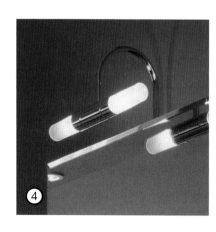

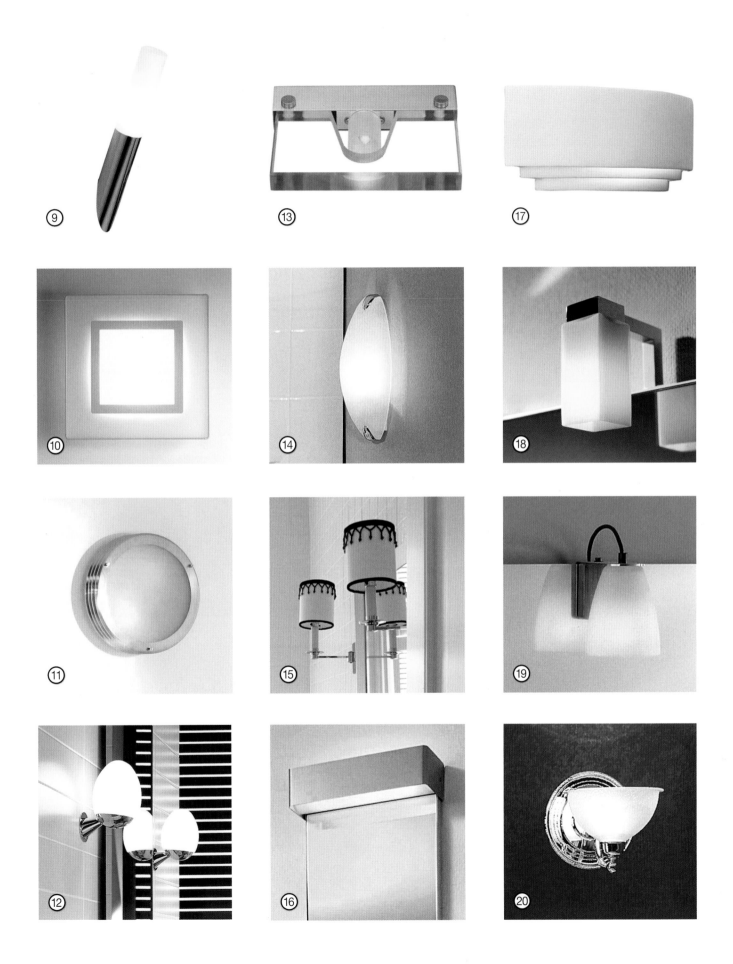

⑨

⑬

⑰

⑩

⑭

⑱

⑪

⑮

⑲

⑫

⑯

⑳

Task Lighting

Task lighting is about practicality, and in a bathroom the lighting around the vanity mirror is crucial. It's important to see yourself as others see you, and that means having adequate, color-correct light that neither romanticizes your reflection nor detracts from it. The most effective solution is to have one fixture on each side of the mirror. Ideally, the fixtures should be separated by about 30 inches (75 cm). This position changes slightly if the room is extremely large or has unusually high ceilings.

If you install a light strip above a mirror, consider using frosted bulbs rather than clear ones. Clear bulbs tend to produce a rather harsh glare that washes the color out of your face.

① A lighted magnifying mirror provides an up-close-and-personal view of your face and makes it easier to shave or apply makeup.

② Shaded light strips on the sides of a mirror provide excellent illumination for a vanity mirror.

③ A partially concealed light panel illuminates this funky mirror.

④ This mirrored cabinet is framed on two sides by color-corrected fluorescent bulbs.

⑤ A strip of frosted bulbs above lights this mirror. Additional illumination is provided by nearby pendant lights and accent lights in the cabinets.

⑥ A vertical fixture throws light to each side of this long, horizontal mirror.

Task lighting of the correct type for vanity mirrors is key. Fluorescent fixtures reduce operating costs because they're extremely energy efficient. The bulbs also last as much as ten times longer than incandescent or halogen bulbs. Many utility companies offer rebates or incentives for consumers who choose fluorescent rather than incandescent fixtures. Check with your electric provider to see whether they have such a program.

The standard objection to fluorescent fixtures is that they sometimes hum or flicker and that the light is not flattering. Both these objections are easily overcome if you shop carefully. Choosing bulbs that use a high-frequency electronic ballast eliminates the hum and flicker. The light from bulbs labeled "color correct" or "warm light" does not have the greenish cast sometimes produced by earlier generations of fluorescents.

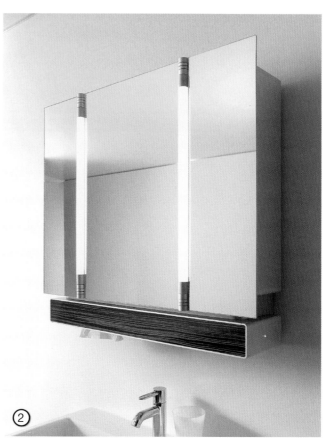

① Light glows from the edges as well as the front of this frameless mirror.

② The doors of this mirrored cabinet are banded with light.

③ A horizontal bar of light extends across this vanity mirror.

④ Fluorescent bulbs frame both sides of this vanity mirror.

⑤ This contemporary mirrored cabinet includes an integral strip of light embedded in the mirror.

⑥ A light fixture is centered at the top of this small vanity mirror.

⑦ This large mirror is surrounded by the warm glow of lights mounted on the back.

⑧ Fluorescent bulbs run the length of each side of this mirrored cabinet.

⑨ The doors of this mirrored cabinet swing open to reveal lighted storage space behind.

⑩ This mirror, which includes an integral magnifying mirror, is lighted from above by a single fluorescent bulb.

⑪ This contemporary lighted mirror includes a unique column of light that projects from the top.

③

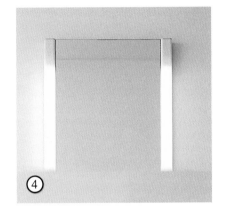

④

⑦

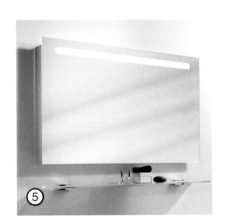

⑤

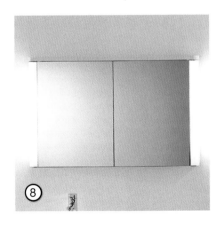

⑧

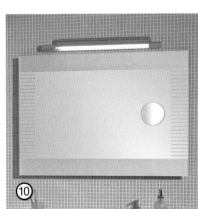

⑩

⑥

⑨

⑪

Decorative Lighting

Special light effects can be dramatic and appealing as a design element. Some people also believe light can soothe emotions and promote physical health.

The effectiveness of chromatherapy, an alternative or "holistic" healing method using colored light, is widely debated. Advocates claim that certain colors and types of light bring out emotional responses that can be predicted and utilized. Skeptics deny the scientific nature of these claims. Studies continue and the debate rages on.

For people who feel their health and emotions are affected by color and light, no further proof is required. Others may not accept the healing nature of colored light, but cannot deny that colored light makes a design statement.

②

①

③

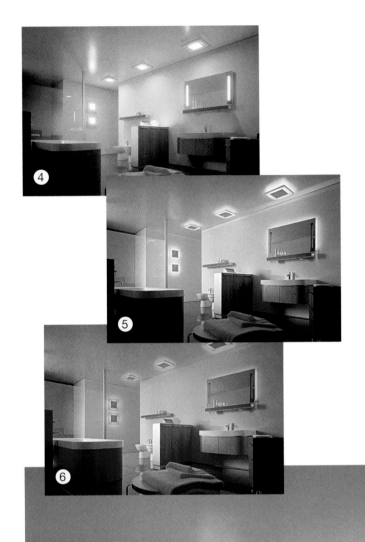

① Colored lights illuminate the water drops streaming from this showerhead.

② Violet light adds an interesting touch to this contemporary faucet.

③ A special fixture washes this glass panel with vivid blue light.

④ An integrated lighting system lets you live inside a rainbow. Here, we see the system's basic white light.

⑤ At the touch of the controls, the system bathes the room in blue light, which many consider soothing.

⑥ Here, the system has been switched to orange light, which is considered invigorating.

⑦ Finally, the system has been set to produce sunny yellow light.

Window Treatments

Well-chosen window treatments contribute to a bathroom's décor, it's true, but they're more than merely decorative. They provide privacy, control light, and temper heat loss or gain. If that weren't enough, they need to do all these things without interfering with the window's operation or the room's ventilation. Selecting window treatments for a bathroom is a matter of balancing functional realities with decorative flair, of matching the features you need with the look you want.

When dressing bathroom windows, the main factors to be considered are privacy, control of the environment, and style.

Bathrooms are private spaces. Privacy may be less of a concern if the house is situated in the middle of a pasture or on the side of a remote mountain, but the average homeowner needs and wants their bathroom windows covered. Blinds, shutters, shades, and opaque fabrics offer excellent levels of privacy. Sheer fabrics may not be adequate, especially at night.

Window treatments are meant to control light and reduce heat gain and loss without interfering with ventilation. Each type has strengths and weaknesses in these areas. For example, draperies provide excellent light control when closed, but block access to fresh air as well as light. Sheer curtains promote ventilation but do little more than obscure direct views of the room. Blinds, on the other hand, can be adjusted to control light without interfering with ventilation, but are not as effective at preventing drafts as other types.

One solution is to dress a window in layers. Pairing blinds with sheer curtains gives you privacy in addition to light control and airiness. Putting a roller shade behind a pair of drapes lets you leave the draperies open for ventilation without concerns over being spotted by the neighbors.

Although they definitely serve specific functions, window treatments offer the opportunity to get creative, and to have fun with colors, textures, and styles. Most window treatments are reasonably priced, especially compared to other elements of a bathroom, such as fixtures and fittings. That means you can take risks, follow interesting trends, or choose daring colors without worrying that you're going to have to live with your decisions forever.

Certain bathroom styles call for certain styles of window treatments. For example, vertical blinds are most at home in contemporary settings. Formal draperies are best suited to traditional rooms. Blinds work with nearly any style, especially when topped by a valance or side panels. Match your window treatment to your bathroom.

Opposite: Sheer window treatments filter the light streaming through the windows surrounding this sunken tub.

Below: A wooden grill covers the large window in this spa-like bathroom. This type of window treatment works best for fixed, rather than operable, windows.

Types, Styles, and Finishes

Any type of window treatment can be used in a bathroom, though some types may need extra care in this environment. Fabric window treatments, for example, should ideally be made from material that can be washed at home.

Blinds provide excellent privacy and light control. They can be opened or closed as necessary, and rarely interfere with ventilation. Blinds are made of vinyl, aluminum, wood, and fabric.

Shutters are hinged, louvered panels. They are great for blocking out or letting in light as desired.

Shades are available in a wide variety of styles. Most offer excellent privacy and light control.

Draperies and curtains are fabric panels that may be opened and closed by means of a system of rods and pulleys or pulled by hand. They are good for keeping heat in and blocking out light.

① Sheer fabric panels filter light in this bathroom but provide little in the way of privacy.

② Shades offer nearly complete privacy. Most are made of fabric and many, such as these Roman shades, are lined.

③ Shutters like these can be folded to the side or extended to cover the windows. When extended, the louvers can be opened or closed to admit more or less light.

④ Blinds can be adjusted easily to control light and ventilation.

⑤ True draperies, such as these, are rare in bathrooms, but their elegance is undeniable.

Drapes and Curtains

Although the words are sometimes used interchangeably, draperies tend to be made of heavier fabric and are designed to be drawn by mechanical means. Curtains typically are made of lighter-weight fabric and designed either to be drawn by hand or remain stationary.

In bathrooms with the right conditions, draperies work beautifully. When made from opaque fabric and lined, they provide exceptional privacy. They also block drafts in the winter.

Curtains are easy to install and don't take as much wall space as draperies. Most are suspended from a simple rod by a rod-pocket casing or by rings or tabs.

① A simple tieback holds this drapery to one side. Releasing it allows the drapery to fall across the entire window.

② Layered over honeycomb shades, these tab-top curtains add warmth and elegance to this master bath.

③ These formal draperies are tucked behind brass rosettes. Rearranging them to provide privacy takes only a moment.

④ Translucent fabric filters light and obscures views in this spa-like atmosphere.

⑤ Yards and yards of brightly colored, gauzy fabric establish a romantic atmosphere in this exotic bathroom.

⑥ When pulled, these drapes sit against a solid wall, leaving the full expanse of the windows open. When drawn, they provide complete privacy and a lovely atmosphere.

⑤

③

①

⑥

Blinds and Shades

Blinds are versatile, affordable, and control light and privacy well. Individual slats can be tilted or the entire blind can be raised and lowered. Blinds are usually made of vinyl, wood, faux wood, aluminum, or natural fibers. Horizontal blinds are common, but vertical blinds are available as well.

Shades, solid pieces of fabric or vinyl, operate in much the same way as blinds. They range from simple to elaborate styles and can be lined to provide privacy or made from sheer fabric to filter the light and obscure views. Most shades can be pulled to any desired height, and some are lowered from the top to admit light even while protecting privacy. Most shades are custom-made to fit each window.

Cords from blinds and shades must be carefully controlled in homes where children are present.

① A simple shade pairs up with etched glass here to provide privacy without sacrificing light. The light fabric dries quickly, an asset for a window treatment in a tub enclosure.

② An opaque-fabric roller shade is positioned to cover half of this window. It can be raised or lowered with a quick tug.

③ The custom-made Roman shade at this window gathers to resemble a valance.

④ Venetian blinds are particularly appropriate in contemporary bathrooms. Separate controls allow you to tilt the slats and raise or lower the blind.

⑤ A custom-made Roman shade covers this exceptionally tall window. Customized shades are great solutions for large or unusual window shapes.

⑥ Narrow wood blinds admit some light here without compromising privacy. High-quality wood blinds stand up to the humid conditions of bathrooms. Lesser-quality products may warp or discolor over time.

⑦ This cellular shade opens from the top down to admit light while protecting the privacy of bathers.

Roller shades are made of opaque vinyl or fabric. They're spring-loaded and snap up or down when pulled. Roller shades typically are quite inexpensive and very efficient at preventing heat gain and loss.

Roman and balloon shades, which are raised or lowered by cords, are custom-made from fabric and usually include linings. They range from simple, flat-fold styles to elaborate cloud styles made from yards and yards of fabric.

Pleated and cellular shades insulate windows to prevent drafts and, when made from opaque material, provide excellent privacy. They operate much like blinds and can be ordered to open and close from the top down or the bottom up.

① Side-pull roller shade
② Center-pull roller shade
③ Roller shade with circular cutouts
④ Roller shade with bottom bar and scalloped tabs
⑤ Roller shade with fringed hem and tasseled pull
⑥ Roller shade with crenelated hem
⑦ Fantail Roman shade
⑧ Pleated Roman shade
⑨ Single-gather festoon shade
⑩ Fan shade
⑪ Cascade shade
⑫ Austrian shade
⑬ Balloon shade
⑭ Tiered cloud shade
⑮ Stagecoach shade
⑯ Roll-up shade
⑰ Sliding panels
⑱ Portiere panel
⑲ Panel fixed with rings
⑳ Fixed lace panel

①

②

③

④

⑤

⑥

⑦

⑧

⑨

⑩

⑪

⑫

⑬

⑭

⑮

⑯

⑰

⑱

⑲

⑳

Shutters

Shutters are traditional window treatments that never go out of style. Wood shutters can be expensive, but new materials are more reasonably priced and may have some advantages over traditional wood shutters. Faux wood, typically plastic, is impervious to water and does not crack or split in extreme temperatures. MDF (medium density fiberboard) shutters are appropriate in bathrooms only if they have high-quality finishes. (Water destroys unprotected MDF.)

Most shutters swing or fold to the sides of the windows. The louvers are controlled, as a group, by means of a rod at the center of the panel.

Home centers and other retailers offer shutters to fit standard window sizes. Many retailers offer custom-made shutters built to specification for your windows.

⑤

① The wide louvers of this custom-made shutter echo the room's wood paneling.

② Plantation shutters are an ideal choice for the clean lines of this contemporary bathroom.

③ The rich wood of this contemporary shutter has been stained to match the vanity.

④ Double shutters like these allow bathers to enjoy the view without compromising their privacy.

⑤ Shutters offer many options for light control and privacy.

⑥ The superior light control of these wood shutters allows bathers to enjoy romantic firelight and chromatherapy, even in the middle of the day.

⑥

Practical Checklist

BUILDING PERMITS

Building-permit requirements change from one municipality to another. At a minimum, a permit is required any time you make changes to the structural framework of your home, or add or subtract elements from the electrical or plumbing system. Before beginning a bathroom remodeling project:

- Check with the local building department to find out if a permit is required and what documentation is necessary to obtain one. Ask for copies of relevant restrictions.
- If your project requires a permit, provide plan drawings or blueprints for review by an inspector. Include details regarding structural support, wiring, and plumbing. During the building process, make arrangements to have the site inspected as necessary.
- If you're building an addition, ask about setback and other restrictions. Have property lines marked and make sure there are no disputes with your neighbors before breaking ground for an addition.
- Before digging for footings or foundations, have all underground utility lines marked. Most areas have one company that provides this service for all underground utility lines.

BUDGETING

Establish a budget for the project before you commit to it. Research all fixtures and building materials thoroughly and comparison-shop based on prices before making purchases, especially for big-ticket items.

If you're hiring a contractor, ask whether there are portions of the project you could do yourself to save money. Many homeowners find doing their own demolition on remodeling projects is a satisfying way to reduce the cost of a project.

DEMOLITION

Remodeling projects often start with demolition. Before you swing that sledgehammer, give some thought to the process. Demolition is not as carefree as it might seem.

Turn off the water supply and power down all electrical circuits in the area. Use a circuit tester to verify that the power is off.

Make arrangements to recycle as many materials as possible, including old fixtures and plumbing lines, especially if they're copper.

Have a dumpster delivered for materials that have to be thrown away.

Older homes sometimes contain materials now considered harmful. If you suspect the presence of hazardous materials, such as lead paint or asbestos, investigate before you begin demolition. If necessary, consult an abatement specialist before disturbing construction materials.

SELECTING FIXTURES

Measure existing spaces, including plumbing locations, precisely, and read all product specifications very carefully before purchasing any fixture. Make sure the configuration of your space and plumbing lines will work with the fixtures you want.

Whenever possible, evaluate fixtures in person. Sit on the toilets and in the tubs; stand in a demo unit of the showers. Whether a fixture is comfortable and convenient is guided largely by personal opinion as well as the size, shape, and physical condition of the user. Don't buy a fixture that doesn't suit you because you were embarrassed to try it out in front of others.

When purchasing large items, such as tubs or shower enclosures, make sure you can get them into the house and through the doors, including the bathroom door.

Consider arranging delivery for heavy or awkward items.

CHOOSING AND HANDLING MATERIALS

Ask how materials should be stored before they're installed. Beadboard and hardwood flooring, for example, should be allowed to rest for several days in the conditions (temperature and humidity levels) under which it will be installed.

Buy moisture-resistant materials for wet zones. For example, you need greenboard rather than drywall for walls in tub or shower alcoves, and cementboard for underlayment beneath ceramic or stone tile. Make sure you select materials appropriate to the conditions found in bathrooms.

Purchase mortars and other adhesives designed for the materials to be installed. For example, ceramic tile requires thin-set mortar and grout.

Buy an extra 10 to 15 percent of the materials to allow for waste and scrap.

When buying tile or other materials that come in color runs or lots, buy at least one extra box and make sure all boxes are labeled with the same run or lot number. Most retailers allow you to return unopened boxes if you buy too much, but it's almost impossible to find more boxes of the same lot if you run out before finishing the project.

Make arrangements to have large, heavy, or delicate items delivered. Open cartons and inspect the products before the delivery person leaves the site. If you discover shipping damage, have the delivery person note that on the receipt. It might be a good idea to take time-stamped photographs right away, too.

DIY OR PROFESSIONAL?
You'll need to decide if you want to design and construct the bathroom yourself or hire professionals to do all or some of the work. To help you make this decision, consider these factors:
- What is your skill level with the types of projects required?
- Do you have the time necessary to devote to completing the project in a reasonable amount of time?
- Do you have the physical strength necessary or access to helpers for the heavy lifting?

If the project is beyond your level of skill or physical strength, requires more time than you have available, or involves major structural changes to the house, hire professionals.

Unless you have experience working with wiring and electricity, it's best to hire an electrician to run cable and make connections. The same goes for plumbing, especially when using copper pipe.

CHOOSING PROFESSIONALS
Bathroom projects require the skills of a variety of professionals and craftspeople.

Architects are licensed professionals who design sound structures that meet local building codes. You may want to hire an architect to draw up blueprints for additions or complex remodeling projects.

General contractors can do any necessary framing, and recruit and manage individual craftspeople for you.

Plumbers install water supply lines, drain/waste/vent systems, fixtures, faucets, and fittings.

Electricians run electrical cable, create circuits, and install switches and receptacles as well as light fixtures and fans.

Designers help you create an aesthetically pleasing arrangement and choose colors, shapes, and textures that complement one another. Choose a designer who specializes in baths and will be experienced.

Finish carpenters do trim work, such as adding cove molding, baseboards, and other architectural details.

HIRING PROFESSIONALS
Get recommendations from family and friends or consult a local contractors' association. Meet with two or three candidates and evaluate your options.
- Ask to see their portfolios and references.
- Get written bids.
- Check references. Ask about their experiences with the contractor and whether they would hire that same person for future jobs.
- Check with the Better Business Bureau to see if there are complaints against any of the candidates.
- Run an Internet search on each candidate to see if you can find any reviews of their work online.

When you decide on a contractor, put your agreement in writing, including work and payment schedules, penalties for non-performance, and extra charges for change orders. Include both a start date and an expected completion date in your written contract.

Make sure you each have a clear understanding of exactly what the project entails, who is responsible for what, and how work will proceed, including the hours and days of the week you can expect workers in your home. If you have special requests, such as asking workers not to smoke near your doors and windows, make sure you discuss those up front.

Glossary

Acrylic: a plastic product that resembles glass, but weighs less and can be molded into shapes. Often used for bathtubs and shower enclosures.

Air-jet tub: a bathtub equipped with one or more pumps that circulate warm air to create a massaging action.

Ambient light: general-purpose light in a room. Typically supplied by natural as well as artificial sources.

Ballast: a device in fluorescent light fixtures that regulates the flow of electricity to the light-producing cathodes.

Ballcock: a valve that controls the water supply entering a toilet tank.

Bidet: low plumbing fixture equipped with a water spray. Used for washing the genital and anal areas.

Blocking: a piece of lumber added between framing studs to add support to the wall.

Building Codes: legal regulations that dictate construction standards in a specific community.

Cast iron: iron cast into shape and then coated with a baked-on enamel. Often used for bathtubs. Exceptionally strong and durable, but heavy.

Caulk: a mastic substance used to seal joints, especially between walls and plumbing fixtures.

Cementboard: a substrate used under tile and stone floors. Designed to remain stable when exposed to moisture.

Ceramic tile: tile made of clay pressed into shape and fired in a kiln.

Console sink: freestanding sink supported by a framework and legs.

Contemporary: a design style that is "characteristic of the present."

Diverter: a valve that stops the flow of water to one location and redirects it to another, such as from a tub spout to a showerhead in a shower/bath combination.

Dry sauna: a sauna operated between 150 and 200°F (65 and 93°C), with no added humidity.

Drywall (also called wallboard or Sheetrock): gypsum panels covered with several layers of paper. Used for interior walls and ceilings.

Enameled steel: medium-weight steel coated with a baked-on enamel. Used for bathtubs.

Far infrared: long light waves in the infrared spectrum, especially those between 10 and 1000 micrometers.

Faucet: spout through which water is delivered to a sink.

Fiberglass: composite product made of polymers reinforced by thin strands of glass. Easily molded. Often used for bathtubs and shower enclosures.

Fittings: the handles or controls attached to a faucet.

Fixtures: sinks, toilets, and bidets.

Floor-warming system: radiant heat system comprised of a mesh of electric resistance wires and a thermostat. Installed in bathroom floors, beneath the floor coverings. Especially valuable for warming tile floors.

Flush lever: handle or button that is pressed to produce the flush of a toilet.

Flush-mounted sink: a sink recessed into the counter to sit flush with the counter's surface.

Framed cabinet: cabinets with face frames that cover the exposed edges of the case. Cabinet doors are set into the frames laid over them.

Frameless cabinet: banding, rather than frames, covers the edges of these cabinets. Doors cover nearly the entire case of frameless cabinets.

Framing member: a term for a single element of construction framework, such as a wall stud.

Friction co-efficient: rating for the slip-resistance of floor coverings.

GFCI or Ground Fault Circuit Interrupter: a safety device engineered to protect electrical circuits from shorts and overloads. GFCI devices detect minute changes in current and shut off power to the circuit before the short can cause injuries. Most Building Codes require that bathroom circuits be protected by GFCIs.

Gravity-fed toilet: toilet that relies on gravity to pull water down into the trap when flushed. Long-time, standard type of toilet.

Greenboard: moisture-resistant drywall product.

Grout: a cement product used to fill crevices between tiles.

Integral sink: a molded basin into a countertop.

Joist: horizontal framing member

that forms support for floors and ceilings.

Linoleum: laminate of linseed oil, wood flour, and pine resins bonded to a jute backing.

Low-voltage: 24-volt current. Transformers step down household current to power low-voltage devices, such as light fixtures and thermostats.

Pedestal sink: a sink that sits on top of a pedestal. Attached to the wall in the same way as a wall-mounted sink.

Period style: design that is faithful to the style of a specific period of history, such as the 18th century.

Pressure-assisted toilet: toilet that relies on a pump to produce vigorous flushing action.

Riser: pipe through which water is delivered to faucets and fittings.

Sauna: a small room fitted with a heating unit to bring the interior space to high temperatures. Often lined with aromatic wood. "Bathing" in a sauna is considered therapeutic.

Self-rimming sink: a sink with rolled edges that rest directly on a countertop.

Shower tower: self-contained unit that includes a pump and thermostat to increase the water pressure and temperature of a multi-head shower.

Solid-surface material: a building material composed of acrylic polymer and alumina trihydrate. Commonly known as Corian, which is a trademarked name from DuPont. Used for countertops, sinks, tubs, and showers.

Steam sauna: room covered with moisture-resistant surfaces and fitted with a steam generator. "Bathing" in a steam sauna is considered therapeutic.

Stud: a vertical framing member of a wall. In houses, studs are 2 x 4 boards spaced 16 inches (40 cm) apart on center.

Task lighting: light supplied to illuminate a specific activity or task.

Tempered glass: a type of safety glass created by exposing standard glass to rapid cycles of heating and cooling. Used for shower enclosures and other settings where standard glass could be dangerous. It is four to five times stronger than annealed (non-tempered) glass. Breaks into relatively harmless, rounded pieces when broken.

Traditional style: design based on the experience of an era, such as Georgian, Victorian, or Arts and Crafts.

Transformer: a device that reduces line voltage from household circuits to a specific low-voltage rating.

Trap: a curved section of pipe that holds standing water to seal drain lines and keep sewer gases from backing up into the house.

Tub spout: large faucet through which water is delivered to a bathtub.

Undermount sink: a sink installed under the edges of the countertop.

Universal design: design sensibility intended to create rooms accessible to users of every size and level of physical ability.

Vanity: cabinet that supports a bathroom sink. Often includes drawers for storage.

Vessel sink: a basin that rests on top of the countertop, which is served by a small drain opening that is covered by the base of the vessel. Often look like bowls or wash basins.

Vinyl flooring: inexpensive, durable floor covering available in large rolls or individual tiles.

Vitreous china: clay product fired at extremely high temperatures: non-porous, impervious to stains, and extremely durable. Often used for sinks and other bathroom fixtures.

Wall-hung sink: a sink mounted directly on the framing of the wall. Often requires additional blocking between wall studs for support.

Wattage: a measure of the rate at which electricity is consumed. Wattage equals voltage x amperes.

Wet room: bathroom where the floors, walls, and ceiling are watertight. Floors are sloped toward a central drain. Showers are not enclosed.

Wet sauna: a sauna operated between 110 and 115°F (43 and 46°C), with high humidity levels. Water added to the heating unit produces steam on demand.

Wet wall: wall that houses plumbing supply and/or drain lines.

Whirlpool tub: a large bathtub equipped with one or more pumps that circulate water and air through individual jets to create a massaging action.

Resource Guide

The following list of manufacturers is meant to be a general guide. It is not intended as a complete listing of products and manufacturers represented in this book.

Airflow
extractor fans
Lancaster Road, Cressex Business Park
High Wycombe, Bucks HP12 3QP
England
Tel: +44 1494 525252
www.airflow.co.uk

American Olean/Daltile
tiles
7834 Hawn Fwy
Dallas, TX 75217
Tel: 214 398 1411
www.americanolean.com

American Standard
bathtubs, faucets, fixtures, furniture, showers
P.O. Box 6820
1 Centennial Plaza
Piscataway, NJ 08855-6820
Tel: 800 442 1902
www.americanstandard-us.com

Anderson Floors
wood flooring
P.O. Box 1155
Clinton, SC 29325
Tel: 864 833 6250
www.andersonfloors.com

Aquaglass
showers
320 Industrial Park Drive
Adamsville, TN 38310
Tel: 800 435 7875
www.aquaglass.com

Aqualisa
showers
The Flyer's Way
Westerham, Kent TN16 1DE
England
Tel: +44 1959 560000
www.aqualisa.com

Aquavision
bathroom TVs
Ibroc House, Essex Road
Hoddesdon, Hertfordshire EN11 0QS
England
Tel: +44 1992 708333
www.aquavision.co.uk

Armstrong
cabinets, linoleum, tiles, vinyl, wood floors
2500 Columbia Ave (17603)
P.O. Box 3001, Lancaster, PA 17604
Tel: 800 233 3823
www.armstrong.com

Artelinae
furniture, sinks
Via dell'Industria, 1
Loc. Santa Barbara
52022 Cavriglia (AR)
Italy
Tel: +39 055 961961
www.artelinea.it

Bonomi
faucets, shower fittings
Via Monsuello
36–2565 Lumezzane S.S. (BS)
Italy
Tel: +39 030 8922121
www.bonomiservice.com

Carina Works
metal tiles and planks
12934 Nutty Brown Rd
Austin, TX 78737
Tel: 800 504 5095
www.carinaworks.com

Ceracasa
tiles and tile murals
Ctra. Castellón-Teruel, Km.19-12110
Alcora Castellón
Spain
Tel: +34 964361611
www.ceracasa.com

Congoleum
vinyl and tiles
P.O. Box 3127
Mercerville, NJ 08619-0127
Tel: 800 274 3266
www.congoleum.com

Deca
accessories, faucets, fixtures, showers
Av. Brasil, 1589
São Paulo SP CEP 01431-001
Brazil
Tel: +55 11 3874 1600
www.deca.com

Dornbracht
faucets, shower fittings
PO Box 1454
D-58584 Iserlohn
Germany
Tel: +49 23 71 433 0
www.dornbracht.com

Duravit
accessories, bathtubs, fixtures, furniture, showers
2205 Northmont Parkway
Suite 200, Duluth, GA 30096
Tel: 770 931 3575
www.duravit.us

Forbo
marmoleum
2 Maplewood Drive, P.O. Box 667
Humboldt Industrial Park
Hazleton, PA 18201
Tel: 1 866 Marmoleum
www.forbolinoleumna.com

Grohe
faucets, shower fittings
241 Covington Drive
Bloomingdale, IL 60108
Tel: 630 582 7711
www.groheamerica.com

Hakatai
tiles
701 Mistletoe Road
Ashland, OR 97520
Tel: 541 552 0855
www.hakatai.com

Hansgrohe
accessories, bathtubs, faucets, showers
1490 Bluegrass Lakes
Parkway, Alpharetta, GA 30004
Tel: 800 488 8119
www.hansgrohe-usa.com

Jado
faucets, shower fittings
6615 West Boston
Chandler, AZ 85226
Tel: 480 951 2675
www.jadousa.com

Kährs International
wood flooring
940 Centre Circle, Suite 1000
Altamonte Springs, FL 32714
Tel: 800 800 5247
www.kahrs.com

Kaldewei
bathtubs, shower trays
Matrix North America
532 Broad Street
2nd Floor, Bloomfield, NJ 07003
Tel: 877 628 7401
www.kaldewei.com

Kohler
bathtubs, faucets, fixtures, furniture,
showers
444 Highland Drive
Kohler, WI 53044
Tel: 800 456 4537
www.us.kohler.com

Laufen
bathtubs, fixtures, furniture,
shower trays
Wahlenstrasse 46, 4242 Laufen
Switzerland
Tel: 866 479 8425
www.laufen.com/usa

Manhattan Showers
showers
Marsden Mill, Brunswick Street
Nelson, Lancashire BB9 0LY
England
Tel: +44 1282 605000
www.manhattanshowers.co.uk

Mannington
carpet, laminate, tiles, vinyl, wood
75 Mannington Mills Road
Salem, NJ 08079
Tel: 800 935 3000
www.mannington.com

Matki
showers
Churchward Road, Yate
Bristol BS37 5PL
England
Tel: +44 1454 322 888
www.matki.co.uk

Paul Lewing Custom Tile
tile murals
4315 Burke Avenue North
Seattle, WA 98103
Tel: 206 547 6591
www.paullewingtile.com

Plain and Fancy
furniture
Oak Street & Route 501
Schaefferstown, PA 17088
Tel: 800 447 9006
www.plainfancycabinetry.com

Plum Door Tile
tile murals
Tel: 941 376 1749
www.plumdoortile.com

Porcelanosa
bathtubs, fixtures, furniture, saunas,
showers, tiles
1301 S State College Blvd, Suite E
Anaheim, CA 92806
Tel: 714 772 3183
www.porcelanosa-usa.com

Porcher
bathtubs, faucets, fixtures, furniture
6615 West Boston Street
Chandler, AZ 85226
Tel: 800 359 3261
www.porcher-us.com

Roca
bathtubs, faucets, fixtures, furniture,
shower trays
Samson Road
Hermitage Industrial Estate
Coalville, Leics LE67 3FP
England
Tel: +44 153 083 0080
www.roca-uk.com

Rohl
faucets, shower fittings
3 Parker
Irvine, CA 92618-1605
Tel: 800 777 9762
www.rohlhome.com

Roman
showers
Whitworth Avenue
Aycliffe Industrial Park
County Durham DL5 6YN
England
Tel: +44 1325 311318
www.roman-showers.com

Sunlight Saunas
saunas
7373 W 107th Street
Overland Park, KS 66212-2547
Tel: 877 292 0020
www.sunlightsaunas.com

Toto
accessories, bathtubs, fixtures, showers
1155 Southern Road
Morrow, GA 30260
Tel: 888 295 8134
www.totousa.com

Venetian Bathrooms
furniture
Gelderd Lane, Leeds LS12 6AL
England
Tel. +44 870 120 8000
www.venetian-bathrooms.co.uk

Villeroy & Boch
faucets, fixtures, furniture, showers, tiles
3 South Middlesex Avenue
Jamesburg NJ 08831
Tel: 609 860 9961
www.villeroy-boch.com

Vogue UK
radiators, towel warmers
Units 6-10
Strawberry Lane Industrial Estate
Strawberry Lane, Willenhall
West Midlands WV13 3RS
England
Tel: +44 1902 387000
www.vogue-uk.com

Waterfront Bathrooms
accessories, faucets, shower fittings
Old Worcester Buildings
Birmingham Road
Redditch, B97 6DY, England
Tel: +44 1527 584244
www.waterfrontbathrooms.com

Wellborn Cabinet Inc
furniture
P.O. Box 1210
Ashland, AL 36251
Tel: 800 336 8040
www.wellborn.com

Index

Acknowledgments

The publishers would like to thank the following companies for their invaluable assistance: Abacus Direct, Airflow, Alexandra Broad Associates, Aquaglass, Aquavision, Carmichael Lynch Spong, DRA Public Relations, Duravit, Grapevine, Grohe, Hakatai, Hansgrohe, Kaldewei, Kohler, Laufen, Parker Hobart, Paul Lewing Custom Tile, Plain and Fancy, Plum Door Tile, Porcelanosa, Publicity Engineers, Roca, Rohl, Roman, Sunlight Saunas, Venetian Bathrooms, Vogue UK, and Wellborn Cabinet Inc

2, 4–5, 6 Laufen

7 Porcelanosa

8–9 1 Laufen; 2 Vogue UK; 3, 4 Bathrooms International

10 1 Laufen; 2 Ideal Standard; 3 Duravit

12–13 1 Laufen; 6 Ideal Standard

14 Andreas von Einsiedel Archive/Designer: Luisella Aramu

15 Laufen

16–17 1 Duravit; 2 C.P. Hart; 3, 4, 6 Porcelanosa; 5 Ambiance Bain

18–19 1 Grant Govier/redcover.com/Designer: R&A Developments Ltd; 2, 3 Laufen; 4 Andreas von Einsiedel Archive/Designer: John Minshaw; 5 Grohe; 6 Verity Welstead/redcover.com; 7 Carlos Dominguez/redcover.com/Shop: Pipe Dreams Ltd

20–21 1 Andreas von Einsiedel Archive/Designer: David Carter; 2 Bathrooms International; 3 Guglielmo Galvin/redcover.com; 4, 6 Ideal Standard; 5 Wellborn Cabinets

22–23 1 Porcelanosa; 2 Jean Maurice/redcover.com; 3 Laufen; 4, 7 Duravit; 5 Ideal Standard

24–25 1 Laufen; 2 Venetian Bathrooms; 3, 4, 6 Porcelanosa; 5 Grohe

26–27 1, 3 Roman; 2 Laufen; 4 Porcelanosa; 5 Winfried Heinze/redcover.com; 6 Venetian Bathrooms

28 Laufen

29 Ideal Standard

30–31 1 David George/redcover.com; 2 Aquavision; 3 Aquaglass; 4 Kohler Co; 5 Duravit

32–33 1 Boundary Bathrooms; 2 Ideal Standard; 3 Porcelanosa; 4 Bieke Claessens/redcover.com; 5 Bathrooms International; 6 David George/redcover.com

34–35 1 Duravit; 2 Bathrooms International; 3 Porcelanosa; 4, 6 Roca; 5 Verity Welstead/redcover.com

36–37 1, 8, 10 Duravit; 2–4, 7 Ideal Standard; 5, 6, 12 Porcelanosa; 9 Laufen; 11 C.P. Hart

38–39 1, 3 Kaldewei; 2 Roca; 4 Daltile; 5 Villeroy & Boch; 6 American Standard; 7 Laufen

40–41 1, 2, 4, 6–12 Roca; 3, 14 Duravit; 5, 13 Kaldewei

42–43 1 Porcelanosa; 2 Villeroy & Boch; 3 Roca; 4 Paul Massey/redcover.com; 5 Tim Evan-Cook/redcover.com; 6 Kaldewei

44–45 1 Ideal Standard; 2, 4 Porcelanosa; 3 Duravit

46–47 1 Roca; 2 Kohler Co; 3–6 Duravit

48 Matki

49 Bathrooms International

50 1 Abacus Direct; 2 Roman

52–53 1 Roman; 2 Hansgrohe Inc; 3 Laufen; 4 Villeroy & Boch; 5 Duravit; 6 Hakatai; 7 Ideal Standard

54–55 1, 6 Roman; 2 Abacus Direct; 3 Ideal Standard; 4 Aquaglass; 5 Porcelanosa

56–57 1, 7, 8 Matki; 2, 5, 6, 9, 19 Ideal Standard; 3, 10 Manhattan Showers; 4, 11, 13–18, 20 Roman; 12 In Design

58–59 1, 4, 15, 16 Hansgrohe Inc; 2, 3 Grohe; 5 Aquaplus Solutions; 6–12 Ideal Standard; 13 Roca; 14 Aqualisa; 17 C.P. Hart

60–61 1 In Design; 2, 3, 5, 7 Porcelanosa; 4 Perrin and Rowe; 6 Ideal Standard; 8 Aqualisa; 9, 17 Grohe; 10–16 Hansgrohe Inc

62–63 1, 6 Aqualisa; 2, 11 Roman; 3 Ideal Standard; 4 Hansgrohe Inc; 5 Perrin and Rowe; 7–10, 12–15 Roca

64–65 1 Hansgrohe Inc; 2 Grohe; 3 Roca; 4 Ideal Standard; 5 Porcelanosa

66–67 1, 3 Hansgrohe Inc; 2, 7 Grohe; 4–6 Roca; 8, 10, 11 Ideal Standard; 9 Porcelanosa

68–69 1, 3, 6 Roman; 2 Hakatai; 4 Abacus Direct; 5 Ideal Standard

70–71 1 Mike Daines/redcover.com; 2 Nick Carter/redcover.com; 3 Lucinda Symons/redcover.com; 4 Roman; 5–16 Roca

72–73 1 © Fernando Bengochea/Beateworks/Corbis; 2, 4, 5 Porcelanosa; 3 Roca

74–75 1 Winfried Heinze/redcover.com; 2, 3 Porcelanosa; 4 Aqualisa; 5 Roman

76–77 1 Evitazonni; 2 Kohler Co; 3 Venetian Bathrooms; 4 Laufen; 5 C.P. Hart

78–79 1, 2, 6 Laufen; 3, 4 Kaldewei; 5 C.P. Hart; 7, 8, 10, 14 Roman; 9, 11–13, 15–18 Roca

80 Ideal Standard

81 © Gareth Brown/Corbis

82–83 1, 5 Porcelanosa; 2 Sunlight Saunas

84–85 1, 2, 4, 5 Porcelanosa; 3 Ideal Standard

86–87 Sunlight Saunas

88–89 1, 5, 6 Porcelanosa; 2 fab-pics/Alamy; 3, 4 Roca

90 Abacus Direct

91 Porcelanosa

92–93 1 Laufen; 2 Grohe; 3 Ideal Standard; 4 Abacus Direct; 5 Perrin and Rowe; 6 Roca

94–95 1 Kohler Co; 2 Ideal Standard; 3, 6 Laufen; 4, 5 Roca; 7 Andrew Twort/redcover.com/Designer: Michael Reeves

96–97 1–4, 9 Roca; 5, 8 Laufen; 6, 10 Duravit; 7 Roman; 11 Porcelanosa; 12 Ideal Standard; 13 Roman

98–99 1 Duravit; 2, 6 Porcelanosa; 3 Grohe; 4 Ideal Standard; 5 Villeroy and Boch

100–101 1–3, 5, 6 Duravit; 4, 8 Laufen; 7 Kohler Co; 9–20 Roca

102–103 1 Roca; 2, 5 Abacus Direct; 3 Ideal Standard; 4 Rohl; 6 Kohler Co; 7 Duravit

104–105 1–3, 6, 7 Duravit; 4 Ideal Standard; 5 Laufen; 8 Bathrooms International; 9–20 Roca

106–107 1 In Design; 2 Kohler Co; 3 Duravit; 4 Johnny Bouchier/redcover.com; 5 Huntley Hedworth/redcover.com; 6 Roca

108–109 1 Aquaplus Solutions; 2, 3, 9 Duravit; 4, 11 Laufen; 5, 12 Porcelanosa; 6 Ideal Standard; 7 Hakatai; 8 Kohler Co; 10 C.P. Hart

110–111 1, 5 Roca; 2, 4 Porcelanosa; 3 Duravit; 6 Laufen

112–113 1, 2 Laufen; 3, 5 Ideal Standard; 4 American Standard

114–115 1, 2, 5, 7, 10 Laufen; 3 American Standard; 4 Abacus Direct; 6, 16 Duravit; 8 © Elizabeth Whiting & Assoc./Corbis; 9, 11–15 Roca

116–117 1 Ideal Standard; 2 Duravit; 3 Venetian Bathrooms; 4 Villeroy and Boch; 5 Roca; 6 Laufen

118–119 1–3, 5, 6 Roca; 4, 8 Ideal Standard; 7, 9–13, 15–19 Laufen; 14 Duravit; 20 Aquaplus Solutions

120 Porcelanosa

121 Laufen

122–123 1 Duravit; 2, 6 Porcelanosa; 3 Kohler Co; 4 Venetian Bathrooms; 5 Roca

124–125 1, 2 Venetian Bathrooms; 3 Wellborn Cabinets; 4 Carlos Dominguez/ redcover.com/Shop: Pipe Dreams Ltd; 5 Ideal Standard; 6 Andreas von Einsiedel Archive/ Designer: Monika Apponyi with special paintwork by Michael Daly

126–127 1 Porcelanosa; 2 Venetian Bathrooms; 3 Wellborn Cabinets; 4–7, 10, 12, 13, 15, 16 Laufen; 8, 11, 14, 19 Duravit; 9, 20 Roca; 17 Ambience Bain; 18 Evitavonni

128–129 1 Kohler Co; 2, 3 Porcelanosa; 4, 5 Laufen; 6 Duravit

130–131 1, 4–6, 10, 13 Laufen; 2, 3, 9, 12, 16 Duravit; 7, 8, 11, 14 Venetian Bathrooms; 15 Porcelanosa; 17 Roca

132–133 1 Roman; 2, 6 Laufen; 3, 4 Porcelanosa; 5 Venetian Bathrooms

134–135 1, 2, 8 Roman; 3, 4, 12, 13, 15 Laufen; 5, 9, 11, 14 Roca; 6 Duravit; 7 Abacus Direct; 10 Venetian Bathrooms

136 Laufen

137 Perrin and Rowe

138–139 1 Rohl; 2 Andreas von Einsiedel Archive/Designer: Precious McBane; 3 Perrin and Rowe; 4 Ideal Standard; 5 Duravit; 6 Abacus Direct; 7 Aquavision

140–141 1, 2 Porcelanosa; 3, 4 Perrin and Rowe; 5 Bathrooms International; 6 Hansgrohe Inc; 7 Aqualisa

142–143 1 Perrin and Rowe; 2 Aquaplus Solutions; 3 Laufen; 4 Hansgrohe Inc; 5–11, 14–16 Roca; 12 Rohl; 13, 18 Aqualisa; 17 Hansgrohe Inc

144–145 1–4, 6, 7, 9–11, 14–18 Roca; 5 Rohl; 8, 19 Perrin and Rowe; 12 Hansgrohe Inc; 13 Bathrooms International; 20 Aqualisa

146–147 1, 2 Duravit; 3 Andreas von Einsiedel Archive/Sproson Barrable Architects; 4 Villeroy and Boch; 5 Bieke Claessens/ redcover.com

148–149 1 Perrin and Rowe; 2 Porcelanosa (except r2c & r3r Perrin and Rowe, r2r Hansgrohe Inc); 3 Porcelanosa (except r1c Perrin and Rowe); 4 Porcelanosa; 5 Porcelanosa (except r1l Hansgrohe Inc, col2top Roca; col2base Perrin and Rowe; 6 Porcelanosa (except 3rd Hansgrohe Inc, 4th Perrin and Rowe)

150–151 1 Porcelanosa; 2, 4 Laufen; 3 Roman; 5 Hansgrohe Inc; 6 Duravit; 7 Aquaplus Solutions

152 Porcelanosa (except 1st Perrin and Rowe, 2nd Hansgrohe Inc, 11th Roca)

153 2 Porcelanosa (except 1st Duravit); 2 Porcelanosa (except 3rd Hansgrohe Inc)

154–155 1 Porcelanosa; 2 Laufen; 3 Roca; 4 Villeroy and Boch; 5 Kaldewei

156 Porcelanosa

157 Duravit

158–159 1, 2 Ideal Standard; 3 Forbo; 4 Porcelanosa; 5 Carina Works; 6 © Spike Powell; Elizabeth Whiting & Assoc./Corbis

160–161 1, 2, 6 Porcelanosa; 3, 4 Daltile; 5 Roman

162–169 Daltile

170–171 1–12 Daltile; 13–20 Carina Works

172–173 1 Ken Hayden/redcover.com/ Architect: Andrea Ballerini; 2 Anthony Harrison/redcover.com; 3, 5 Paul Lewing Custom Tile; 4 Plain and Fancy/Ceracasa

178–179 1 Porcelanosa; 2 Roman; 3 Duravit; 4 Grohe; 5 Andreas von Einsiedel Archive/ Designer: Anthony Brooks with special paintwork by Michael Daly; 6 Andreas von Einsiedel Archive/Designer: Elizabeth Parsons

180–181 1 Porcelanosa; 2 Ideal Standard; 3 Abacus Direct; 4, 6 Laufen; 5 Hansgrohe Inc

182–183 1, 7, 9 Mannington; 2, 12, 16 Award Hardwood Floors; 3, 4, 6, 8, 10, 11, 13–15, 18, 20 Kährs; 5 Teragren; 17, 19 Anderson Floors

184–185 1 Armstrong; 2 Anthony Harrison/ redcover.com; 3, 4 Roman

186–187 1 Forbo; 2–7, 9–21 Congoleum; 8 Armstrong

188–189 Armstrong

190–191 1–4 Ideal Standard; 5–8 Duravit

192 Vogue UK

193 Airflow

194–195 1, 4 Vogue UK; 2 Andreas von Einsiedel Archive/ Rose Uniacke Interiors; Andreas von Einsiedel Archive/Vitznau Park Hotel; 5 Ashley Morrison/redcover.com; 6 Laufen; 7 Ken Hayden/redcover.com

196–197 1 Roman; 2–6 Vogue UK

198–199 Vogue UK

200–201 1 Bieke Claessens/redcover.com; 2 Winifried Heinze/redcover.com; 3 Chris Tubbs/redcover.com; 4 Tom Scott/redcover. com; 5, 6 Airflow

202 Laufen

203 Andreas von Einsiedel Archive/Designer: Kate Earle @ Todhunter-Earle Interiors

204–205 1 Grant Govier/redcover.com/ Designer: R&A Developments Ltd; 2 C.P. Hart; 3, 4, 6 Roca; 5 Andreas von Einsiedel Archive/Designer: Alison Henry Interiors;

7 Laufen

206–207 1 Grant Govier/redcover.com; 2 In Design; 3 Matki; 4, 5 Hakatai; 6 David Hiscock/redcover.com

208–209 1 Andreas von Einsiedel Archive/ Designer: Elizabeth Cawi; 2 Andreas von Einsiedel Archive/Designer: Linda Burgess; 3 Grey Crawford/redcover.com; 4 Andreas von Einsiedel Archive/Designer: Gerd and Christine Sander; 5 Andreas von Einsiedel Archive/Smiros & Smiros Architects; 6 Ambiance Bain

210–211 1, 5, 9, 13, 17 J Baker; 2 Andreas Karelias/Fotolia.com; 3, 4, 7, 14, 16, 18 Laufen; 6 Kohler Co; 8 Jean Maurice/ redcover.com; 10 Duravit; 11 Venetian Bathrooms; 12 Villeroy and Boch; 15 Andreas von Einsiedel Archive/ Designer: Constanze von Unruh; 19 Roca; 20 Aquaglass

212–213 1 Fabio Lombrici/redcover.com/ Architect: Juan Carlos Sanchez; 2 Andreas von Einsiedel Archive/Designer: Candy & Candy; 3 C.P. Hart; 4, 6 Laufen; 5 Wellborn Cabinets

214–215 1 Kohler Co; 2, 4, 6, 7, 9 Duravit; 3, 8, 11 Laufen; 5 Schneider; 10 Roca

216–217 1 Laufen; 2 Porcelanosa; 3–7 Duravit

218 © Massimo Listri/Corbis

219 Bathrooms International

220–221 1, 4 Kaldewei; 2 Bieke Claessens/ redcover.com; 3 Andreas von Einsiedel Archive/Designer: Constanze von Unruh; 4 Bieke Claessens/redcover.com

222–223 1 American Standard; 2 © Dan Forer/Beateworks/Corbis; 3 Andreas von Einsiedel Archive/Designer: Annie Constantine; 4 Rohl; 5 Mel Yates/ redcover.com; 6 © Douglas Hill/Beateworks/ Corbis

224–225 1 redcover.com; 2 Simon McBride/ redcover.com; 3 Andreas von Einsiedel Archive/Designer: Stephanie Hoppen; 4 Villeroy and Boch; 5 Andreas von Einsiedel Archive/Designer: Stephanie Kelly Hoppen; 6 Duravit; 7 Duette® honeycomb shades from Hunter Douglas

228–229 1 Andreas von Einsiedel Archive/ Architects: Project Orange; 2 Andreas von Einsiedel Archive/Designer: Candy & Candy; 3 Duravit; 4 Niall McDiarmid/redcover.com; 5 Andreas von Einsiedel Archive/Designer: Kelly Hoppen; 6 Kohler Co